ECONOMIC ISSUES, PROBLEMS AND PERSPECTIVES

THE LONG-TERM BUDGET OUTLOOK: FEDERAL BUDGET SPENDING AND REVENUE SCENARIOS

Economic Issues, Problems and Perspectives

Additional books in this series can be found on Nova's website under the Series tab.

Additional E-books in this series can be found on Nova's website under the E-books tab.

American Political, Economic, and Security Issues

Additional books in this series can be found on Nova's website under the Series tab.

Additional E-books in this series can be found on Nova's website under the E-books tab.

ECONOMIC ISSUES, PROBLEMS AND PERSPECTIVES

THE LONG-TERM BUDGET OUTLOOK: FEDERAL BUDGET SPENDING AND REVENUE SCENARIOS

JESSICA C. ANDERSON
EDITOR

Nova Science Publishers, Inc.
New York

For permission to use material from this book please contact us:
Telephone 631-231-7269; Fax 631-231-8175
Web Site: http://www.novapublishers.com

LIBRARY OF CONGRESS CATALOGING-IN-PUBLICATION DATA

The long-term budget outlook : federal budget spending and revenue scenarios
/ editor, Jessica C. Anderson.
p. cm.
Includes index.
ISBN 978-1-61122-190-9 (hardcover)
1. Budget--United States--Forecasting. 2. Government spending
policy--United States. 3. United States--Appropriations and
expenditures--Forecasting. I. Anderson, Jessica C.
HJ2051.L665 2010
336.73--dc22
2010041322

Published by Nova Science Publishers, Inc. † New York

CONTENTS

PREFACE

Recently, the federal government has been recording the largest budget deficits, as a share of the economy, since the end of World War II. As a result of those deficits, the amount of federal debt held by the public has surged. At the end of 2008, that debt equaled 40 percent of the nation's annual economic output, as measured by GDP, a little above the 40 year average of 36 percent. Since then, large budget deficits have caused debt held by the public to shoot upward. As the economy recovers and the policies adopted to counteract the recession and the financial turmoil phase out, budget deficits will probably decline markedly in the next few years. But over the long term, the budget outlook is daunting. This book examines the long-term budget outlook with a focus on federal budget spending and revenue scenarios.

Chapter 1- Recently, the federal government has been recording the largest budget deficits, as a share of the economy, since the end of World War II. As a result of those deficits, the amount of federal debt held by the public has surged. At the end of 2008, that debt equaled 40 percent of the nation's annual economic output (as measured by gross domestic product, or GDP), a little above the 40-year average of 36 percent. Since then, large budget deficits have caused debt held by the public to shoot upward; the Congressional Budget Office (CBO) projects that federal debt will reach 62 percent of GDP by the end of this year—the highest percentage since shortly after World War II. The sharp rise in debt stems partly from lower tax revenues and higher federal spending related to the recent severe recession and turmoil in financial markets. However, the growing debt also reflects an imbalance between spending and revenues that predated those economic developments.

Chapter 2- Following the financial crisis, the budget deficit reached 10% of GDP in 2009, a level that cannot be sustained in the long run. Concerns about long-term fiscal sustainability depend on the projected future path of the budget, absent future policy changes. The retirement of the baby boomers, rising life expectancy, and the rising cost of medical care result in projections of large and growing budget deficits over the next several decades. Social Security outlays are projected to rise from 4.8% of gross domestic product (GDP) today to 6.0% of GDP in 2035, and Medicare and Medicaid outlays are projected to rise from 5.3% today to as much as 10.0% of GDP in 2035 and 12.7% of GDP in 2050. These increases in spending are not expected to subside after the baby boomers have passed away. Without any corresponding rise in revenues, this spending path would lead to unsustainably large and persistent budget deficits, which would push up interest rates and the trade deficit, crowd out private investment spending, and ultimately cause fiscal crisis.

Chapter 3- As economic recovery continues, the focus on the federal budget has shifted, in part, towards deficit reduction. In fiscal year (FY) 2009, the federal budget deficit, relative to the size of the economy, reached a level not seen since the end of World War II. Deficit levels are projected to remain elevated through FY20 11. The budget deficit for FY20 11, according to CBO's analysis of the President's budget, is projected to be $1,342 billion. In his FY20 11 budget, the President made several proposals to curb spending, while acknowledging that additional steps are needed to achieve long-term fiscal stability.

In: The Long-Term Budget Outlook
Editor: Jessica C. Anderson
ISBN: 978-1-61122-190-9

Chapter 1

THE LONG-TERM BUDGET OUTLOOK

Congressional Budget Office

SUMMARY

Recently, the federal government has been recording the largest budget deficits, as a share of the economy, since the end of World War II. As a result of those deficits, the amount of federal debt held by the public has surged. At the end of 2008, that debt equaled 40 percent of the nation's annual economic output (as measured by gross domestic product, or GDP), a little above the 40-year average of 36 percent. Since then, large budget deficits have caused debt held by the public to shoot upward; the Congressional Budget Office (CBO) projects that federal debt will reach 62 percent of GDP by the end of this year—the highest percentage since shortly after World War II. The sharp rise in debt stems partly from lower tax revenues and higher federal spending related to the recent severe recession and turmoil in financial markets. However, the growing debt also reflects an imbalance between spending and revenues that predated those economic developments.

As the economy recovers and the policies adopted to counteract the recession and the financial turmoil phase out, budget deficits will probably decline markedly in the next few years. But over the long term, the budget outlook is daunting. The retirement of the baby-boom generation portends a significant and sustained increase in the share of the population receiving benefits from Social Security, Medicare, and Medicaid. Moreover, per capita spending for health care is likely to continue rising faster than spending per person on other goods and services for many years (although the magnitude of that gap is very uncertain). Without significant changes in government policy, those factors will boost federal outlays sharply relative to GDP in coming decades under any plausible assumptions about future trends in the economy, demographics, and health care costs.

The Outlook for Major Health Care Programs and Social Security

CBO projects that if current laws do not change, federal spending on major mandatory health care programs will grow from roughly 5 percent of GDP today to about 10 percent in 2035 and will continue to increase thereafter.[1] Those projections include all of the effects of the recently enacted health care legislation, which is expected to increase federal spending in the next 10 years and for most of the following decade.[2] By 2030, however, that legislation will slightly reduce federal spending for health care if all of its provisions are fully implemented, CBO projects. That reduction in the level of spending in 2030 yields lower projections of health care spending in the longer term—even though, owing to the great uncertainties involved in projecting such spending many decades in the future, enactment of the legislation did not cause CBO to change its estimates of longer-term growth rates for spending on the government's health care programs.

Under current law, spending on Social Security is also projected to rise over time as a share of GDP, albeit much less dramatically. CBO projects that Social Security spending will increase from less than 5 percent of GDP today to about 6 percent in 2030 and then stabilize at roughly that level.

All told, CBO projects, the aging of the population and the rising cost of health care will cause spending on the major mandatory health care programs and Social Security to grow from roughly 10 percent of GDP today to about 16 percent of GDP 25 years from now if current laws are not changed. (By comparison, spending on *all* of the federal government's programs and activities, excluding interest payments on debt, has averaged 18.5 percent of GDP over the past 40 years.) To put U.S. fiscal policy on a sustainable path, lawmakers would have to substantially reduce the growth in outlays for those programs relative to the amounts that CBO is projecting—or else match that growth with equivalent declines in other federal spending, corresponding increases in federal revenues, or some combination of the two.

Alternative Long-Term Scenarios

In this chapter, CBO presents the long-term budget picture under two scenarios that embody different assumptions about future policies governing federal revenues and spending. Budget projections grow increasingly uncertain as they extend farther into the future, so this chapter focuses largely on the next 25 years. However, because considerable interest exists in the longer-term outlook, figures showing projections through 2080 are presented in Appendix A, and associated data are available on CBO's Web site.

The first long-term budget scenario used in this analysis, the *extended-baseline scenario,* adheres closely to current law. It incorporates CBO's current estimate of the impact of the recently enacted health care legislation on revenues and mandatory spending. (That estimate is unchanged from the one that CBO and the staff of the Joint Committee on Taxation published in March, when the legislation was being considered.) Under this scenario, the expiration of most of the tax cuts enacted in 2001 and 2003, the growing reach of the alternative minimum tax, and the way in which the tax system interacts with economic growth would result in steadily higher average tax rates. Those rising rates, combined with the tax provisions of the recent health care legislation, would push total revenues to 23 percent of GDP by 2035—much higher than has typically been seen in recent decades—and to larger percentages thereafter. At the same time, government spending on everything other than the major mandatory health care programs, Social Security, and interest on federal debtactivities such as national defense and a wide variety of domestic programs—would decline to the lowest percentage of GDP since before World War II.

That significant increase in revenues and decrease in the relative importance of other spending would offset much—though not all—of the rise in spending on health care programs and Social Security. As a result, debt would increase from its already high levels relative to GDP, as would the required interest payments on that debt. Federal debt held by the public would grow from an estimated 62 percent of GDP this year to about 80 percent by 2035. Interest payments, which absorb federal resources that could otherwise be used to pay for government services, currently amount to more than 1 percent of GDP; under this scenario, they would rise to 4 percent of GDP (or one-sixth of federal revenues) by 2035.

The budget outlook is much bleaker under the *alternative fiscal scenario*, which incorporates several changes to current law that are widely expected to occur or that would modify some provisions of law that might be difficult to sustain for a long period. In this scenario, CBO assumed that Medicare's payment rates for physicians would gradually increase (which would not happen under current law) and that several policies enacted in the recent health care legislation that would restrain growth in health care spending would not continue in effect after 2020. In addition, under the alternative scenario, spending on activities other than the major mandatory health care programs, Social Security, and interest would fall below the average level of the past 40 years relative to GDP, though not as low as under the extended-baseline scenario. More important, CBO assumed for this scenario that most of the provisions of the 2001 and 2003 tax cuts would be extended, that the reach of the alternative minimum tax would be kept close to its historical extent, and that over the longer run, tax law would evolve further so that revenues would remain at about 19 percent of GDP, near their historical average.

Under that combination of policy assumptions, federal debt would grow much more rapidly than under the extended-baseline scenario. With significantly lower revenues and higher outlays, debt would reach 87 percent of GDP by 2020, CBO projects. After that, the growing imbalance between revenues and noninterest spending, combined with spiraling interest payments, would swiftly push debt to unsustainable levels. Debt as a share of GDP would exceed its historical peak of 109 percent by 2025 and would reach 185 percent in 2035.

Neither of those scenarios represents a prediction by CBO of what policies will be in effect during the next several decades. The policies adopted in coming years will surely differ from those assumed for the scenarios. (And even if the assumed policies were adopted, their economic and budgetary consequences would certainly differ from those projected in this chapter.) Nevertheless, these projections, encompassing two very different sets of policy assumptions, provide a clear indication of the serious nature of the fiscal challenge facing the nation.

The Impact of Growing Deficits and Debt

In fact, CBO's projections understate the severity of the long-term budget problem because they do not incorporate the significant negative effects that accumulating substantial amounts of additional federal debt would have on the economy:

- Large budget deficits would reduce national saving, leading to higher interest rates, more borrowing from abroad, and less domestic investment—which in turn would lower income growth in the United States.
- Growing debt would also reduce lawmakers' ability to respond to economic downturns and other challenges.
- Over time, higher debt would increase the probability of a fiscal crisis in which investors would lose confidence in the government's ability to manage its budget, and the government would be forced to pay much more to borrow money.

Keeping deficits and debt from growing to unsustainable levels would require raising revenues as a percentage of GDP significantly above past levels, reducing outlays sharply relative to CBO's projections, or some combination of those approaches. Making such changes while economic activity and employment remain well below their potential levels would probably slow the economic recovery. However, the sooner that long-term changes to spending and revenues are agreed on, and the sooner they are carried out once the economic weakness ends, the smaller will be the damage to the economy from growing federal debt. Earlier action would require more sacrifices by earlier generations to benefit future generations, but it would also permit smaller or more gradual changes and would give people more time to adjust to them.

The federal government has recently been recording the largest budget deficits, relative to the size of the economy, since 1945. As a result, the amount of federal debt held by the public has surged. Debt is expected to equal 62 percent of the economy's annual output, or gross domestic product (GDP), at the end of this fiscal year, up from 40 percent at the end of 2008. That sharp deterioration in the fiscal situation reflects several factors: an imbalance between spending and revenues that predated the recent recession and the turmoil in financial markets; a decline in tax revenues and an increase in spending on benefit programs caused by those economic problems; and the costs of federal policies enacted in response to the problems.

If current laws were to remain unchanged, the budget deficit would drop markedly as a percentage of GDP in the next few years, the Congressional Budget Office (CBO) projects, and federal debt held by the public would stabilize at about 67 percent of GDP for the next decade.[3] Those baseline projections, however, understate the budget deficits that would arise if policies that are in effect now or have been in effect recently were extended, instead of implementing what current laws specify for future years. Specifically, if most provisions of the tax cuts enacted in 2001 and 2003 were extended rather than allowed to expire as scheduled, if provisions designed to limit the reach of the alternative minimum tax (AMT) were also extended, and if annual appropriations kept pace with the growth of GDP, by 2020 the budget deficit would be growing steadily. In that case, debt held by the public would reach almost 90 percent of GDP in 2020.

Looking beyond the next decade, the fiscal outlook worsens further. Although long-term budget projections are highly uncertain, if current laws were followed, the aging of the population and rising costs for health care would almost certainly cause federal spending to rise sharply relative to GDP. Federal revenues would increase to significantly higher levels under current law than have ever been seen in the United States, but they would still fall short of spending, according to CBO's long-term projections. Consequently, federal debt would grow relative to the size of the economy after the next decade. By 2035, it would equal 79 percent of GDP—the highest percentage in U.S. history except for the period between 1944 and 1950.

An alternative scenario presented in this chapter incorporates several changes to current law that are widely expected to occur or that would modify some provisions of law that might be difficult to sustain for a long period. If such changes occurred—maintaining what some analysts might consider "current policy" as opposed to current law—revenues would increase much more slowly than spending, and federal debt would balloon to 185 percent of GDP by 2035. As debt grows, so does the burden of paying interest on it; thus, under that alternative scenario, interest outlays would rise from about 1 percent of GDP today to 9 percent by 2035. With still larger amounts of debt projected for later years under that scenario, such a path for federal borrowing would clearly be unsustainable.

Moreover, the projected outcomes under both scenarios do not include the harmful effects that rising debt would have on economic growth and interest rates. If those effects were taken into account, projected debt would increase even faster.

If policymakers are to put the nation on a sustainable budgetary path, they will need to let revenues increase substantially as a percentage of GDP, decrease spending significantly from projected levels, or adopt some combination of those two approaches. With economic activity and employment currently well below the levels that could be achieved by fully utilizing the nation's labor force and capital stock, raising revenues or curbing spending immediately would probably slow the economic recovery. However, the sooner that long-term changes to spending and revenues are agreed on, and the sooner they are implemented after the period of economic weakness, the smaller will be the damage to the economy from rising federal debt.

Alternative Scenarios for the Long-Term Budget Outlook

In this chapter, CBO presents two sets of long-term budget projections that are based on differing assumptions about future policy (see Table 1-1):

- The *extended-baseline scenario* adheres most closely to current law. It follows CBO's March 2010 baseline budget projections (adjusted for the effects of recently enacted health care legislation) for the next decade and then extends the baseline concept beyond that 10-year window.[4] This scenario incorporates CBO's current estimate of the impact of the recent health care legislation on revenues and mandatory spending; that estimate is unchanged from March. The current-law assumption of the extended-baseline scenario implies that many adjustments that lawmakers have routinely made in the past—such as changes to the AMT and to the Medicare program's payments to physicians—will not be made again.[5] Because of the structure of cur-rent tax law, federal revenues would grow significantly faster than GDP over the long run under this scenario.
- The *alternative fiscal scenario* embodies several possible changes to current law that would continue certain tax and spending policies that people have grown accustomed to (because the policies are in place now or have been in place recently). Versions of some of the changes assumed in the scenario—such as those related to the AMT and Medicare's payments to physicians—have regularly been enacted in the past. Those and certain other changes included in the scenario—such as changes related to the tax cuts enacted in 2001 and 2003—are widely expected to be made in some form over the next few years. If they are, they will receive special treatment under the Statutory PayAs-You-Go Act of 2010 (Public Law 111-139), which excludes some of the costs of such changes from the law's budget enforcement rules. (For details, see Box 1-1.)

  After 2020, the alternative fiscal scenario also incorporates potential modifications to several provisions of current law that might be difficult to sustain for a long period. Those provisions include certain restraints on the growth of spending for Medicare and indexing provisions that will slow the growth of subsidies for health insurance coverage. Other provisions of current law, if continued, would cause tax revenues as a percentage of GDP to ultimately rise well above the levels that U.S. taxpayers have seen in the past. Therefore, the alternative fiscal scenario also incorporates unspecified changes in tax law that would keep revenues constant as a share of GDP after 2020. Together, the changes in the alternative fiscal scenario represent one interpretation of what it would mean to continue today's underlying fiscal policy. However, different analysts might perceive the underlying intention of current policy differently.

Table 1.1. Assumptions About Spending and Revenues Underlying CBO's Long-Term Budget Scenarios

	Extended-Baseline Scenario	Alternative Fiscal Scenario
Assumptions About Spending		
Medicare	As scheduled under current law	As scheduled under current law, except that payment rates for physicians grow with the Medicare economic index (rather than at the lower rates of the sustainable growth rate mechanism) and that after 2020, several policies that would restrain spending growth are assumed not to be in effect
Medicaid and Exchange Subsidies	As scheduled under current law	As scheduled under current law, except that after 2020, a policy that would slow the growth of subsidies for health insurance coverage is assumed not to be in effect
CHIP	As projected in CBO's baseline through 2020; adjusted for growth in per capita GDP and the size of the under-18 population thereafter	As projected in CBO's baseline through 2020; adjusted for growth in per capita GDP and the size of the under-18 population thereafter
Social Security	As scheduled under current law	As scheduled under current law
Other Noninterest Spending	As projected in CBO's baseline through 2020; remaining at the 2020 level as a share of GDP	As projected in CBO's baseline through 2013; remaining at the 2010 level as a share of GDP (minus

Table 1-1. (Continued)

	Extended-Baseline Scenario	Alternative Fiscal Scenario
	thereafter, except that some refundable tax credits, Medicare premiums, and certain payments by states to Medicare are as scheduled under current law	stimulus and related spending) thereafter, except that some refundable tax credits, Medicare premiums, and certain payments by states to Medicare are as sched-uled under current law
Assumptions About Revenues		
Individual Income Taxes	As scheduled under current law	Through 2020, tax cuts from EGTRRA and JGTRRA are extended (except for rate reductions that apply to high-income taxpayers) and AMT relief is extended; thereafter, individual income taxes are adjusted to keep total revenues constant as a share of GDP
Payroll Taxes	As scheduled under current law	As scheduled under current law
Corporate Income Taxes	As scheduled under current law through 2020; remaining constant as a share of GDP thereafter	As scheduled under current law through 2020; remaining constant as a share of GDP thereafter
Excise Taxes	As scheduled under current law	As scheduled under current law though 2020; remaining constant as a share of GDP thereafter
Estate and Gift Taxes	As scheduled under current law	2009 tax rates and exemption amount (adjusted for inflation) continue through 2020; revenues are constant as a share of GDP thereafter
Other Sources of Revenue	As scheduled under current law through 2020; remaining constant as a share of GDP thereafter	As scheduled under current law through 2020; remaining constant as a share of GDP thereafter

Source: Congressional Budget Office.

Notes: The extended-baseline scenario adheres closely to current law, following CBO's 10-year baseline budget projections through 2020 (with adjustments for the recently enacted health care legislation) and then extending the baseline concept for the rest of the longterm projection period. The alternative fiscal scenario incorporates several changes to current law that are widely expected to occur or that would modify some provisions that might be difficult to sustain for a long period.

CHIP = Children's Health Insurance Program; GDP = gross domestic product; EGTRRA = Economic Growth and Tax Relief Reconciliation Act of 2001; JGTRRA = Jobs and Growth Tax Relief Reconciliation Act of 2003; AMT = alternative minimum tax.

The projections in this chapter understate the size of the budgetary shortfalls that would be likely to result from such fiscal policies. For the purposes of the projections, CBO assumed stable economic conditions after 2020— in particular, a constant real (inflation-adjusted) interest rate on federal debt and steady growth rates for real wages and output. That approach omits the pressures that a rise in debt as a percentage of GDP would have on real interest rates and economic growth. It also omits the impact that higher effective marginal tax rates and the increasing value of government benefits would have on incentives to work and save.[6]

The Extended-Baseline Scenario

Under CBO's current-law scenario, primary spending— all spending except interest payments on federal debt— would drop relative to GDP in the next few years, level out for the rest of the decade, and grow significantly in later decades. The severe recession and financial turmoil, as well as federal policies implemented in response to them, pushed primary spending to 23 percent of GDP last year, the highest level since World War II. Those factors will keep spending at roughly the same level in 2010 and 2011, CBO projects. However, as the economy recovers and the budgetary effects of those policies diminish, primary spending is projected to decline to 20 percent of GDP and remain near that level through 2020. In subsequent years, primary spending would follow a long upward trajectory under the extended-baseline scenario, reaching 24 percent of GDP in 2035 (see the top panel of Figure 1-1) and 30 percent in 2080.[7] (This chapter focuses on primary spending because growth in debt as a share of GDP is determined mainly by the relationship between revenues and primary outlays.)

Revenues would also rise considerably under current law; by the 2020s, they would reach higher levels relative to the size of the economy than ever recorded in the nation's history. Currently about 15 percent of GDP, revenues would jump to 19 percent in 2012 as the economic recovery increased taxable income, and thus tax receipts; as most of the tax reductions enacted in 2001 and 2003 expired at the end of 2010 as scheduled; and as the reach of the AMT expanded greatly, because (unlike most of the tax code) the dollar amounts of its parameters do not increase with inflation. In subsequent years, revenues would continue to rise relative to GDP, for three main reasons. First, ongoing increases in real income would push taxpayers into higher tax brackets. Second, ongoing inflation, even if modest, would cause more people to owe tax under the AMT. And third, the recently enacted excise tax on certain high-premium health insurance plans would have a growing effect on revenues. Taken together, those factors would cause federal revenues to grow faster than the economy, reaching 23 percent of GDP in 2035 and 30 percent in 2080.

BOX 1-1. THE STATUTORY PAY-AS-YOU-GO ACT OF 2010

In February 2010, lawmakers enacted a new version of some of the budget enforcement procedures that were in effect in the 1 990s. The Statutory Pay-AsYou-Go Act of 2010 (Public Law 111-139) aims to make sure that most new legislation affecting revenues or mandatory spending does not increase federal budget deficits. The law requires the Congressional Budget Office (CBO) to estimate the potential budgetary effects of proposed legislation that is subject to the new procedures; it also requires the Office of Management and Budget to keep a running tally of the average annual budgetary impact of any such legislation that is enacted.[1] If, at the end of a Congressional session, the tally shows a net cost for the budget year from such legislation, the Administration must order a sequestration—canceling certain already enacted mandatory funding—to cover that cost.

Under current law, some payment rates and tax rates will change significantly if they are not extended at their present levels. The Statutory Pay-As-You-Go Act provides special treatment for legislation that does the following:

- Amends or supersedes the system for updating Medicare's payments to physicians;
- Continues the parameters of the estate and gift taxes at their 2009 levels, adjusted for inflation;
- Adjusts the exemption amounts under the alternative minimum tax to keep the number of people affected by that tax at the same level as in 2008; or
- Extends certain expiring provisions of the Economic Growth and Tax Relief Reconciliation Act of 2001 and the Jobs and Growth Tax Relief Reconciliation Act of 2003 for taxpayers who currently make less than $250,000 (in the case of couples filing joint returns) or $200,000 (in the case of single filers).

Such legislation is subject to the new law's pay-as- you-go rules. But the tally of the budgetary effects of the legislation must reflect specific "current-policy adjustments" that reduce the recorded cost of those changes. The authority to allow for such adjustments expires on January 1, 2012.

[1] The Statutory Pay-As-You-Go Act does not apply to discretionary funding provided in appropriation acts or to any legislative provision that the Congress designates as an emergency requirement.

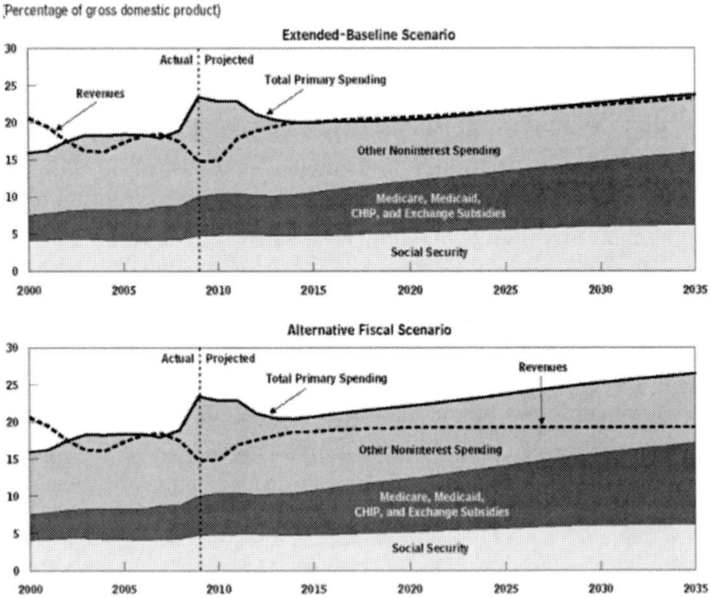

Source: Congressional Budget Office.

Notes: Primary spending refers to all spending other than interest payments on federal debt.

The extended-baseline scenario adheres closely to current law, following CBO's 10-year baseline budget projections through 2020 (with adjustments for the recently enacted health care legislation) and then extending the baseline concept for the rest of the longterm projection period. The alternative fiscal scenario incorporates several changes to current law that are widely expected to occur or that would modify some provisions that might be difficult to sustain for a long period. (For details, see Table 1-1 on page 3.)

CHIP = Children's Health Insurance Program.

Figure 1.1. Revenues and Primary Spending, by Category, Under CBO's Long-Term Budget Scenarios.

However, even with revenues rising to those levels (and omitting the economic effects of such increases), the budget would still be out of balance over the long term under the extended-baseline scenario. As a result, the deficit (including interest costs) would equal about 4 percent of GDP in 2035, and federal debt held by the public would continue to accumulate, rising to 79 percent of GDP in 2035 and larger percentages thereafter.

The Alternative Fiscal Scenario

Under the alternative fiscal scenario, primary spending would be 1.6 percentage points higher as a share of GDP in 2020 than under the extended-baseline scenario (see the bottom panel of Figure 1-1). That difference would grow in later years. The higher spending stems from several assumptions of the alternative fiscal scenario: that lawmakers would act to raise Medicare's payments to physicians; that lawmakers would not allow various restraints on the growth of costs for Medicare and for health insurance subsidies to have their full effect in the decade after 2020; and that federal spending for things other than major mandatory programs or interest payments would be similar to typical recent levels as a percentage of GDP (rather than declining through 2020, as under the extended-baseline scenario).[8]

On the revenue side, the alternative fiscal scenario incorporates the assumptions that most of the cuts in individual income taxes enacted in 2001 and 2003 that are now scheduled to expire in 2011 (except the lower rates applying to high-income taxpayers) are extended through 2020; that relief from the AMT, which expired after 2009, continues through 2020; and that the 2009 parameters of the estate tax (adjusted for inflation) apply through 2020. Thereafter, revenues are assumed to remain at their 2020 level of just over 19 percent of GDP, about a percentage point above the average of the past 40 years. That revenue path, combined with the spending policies described above, would produce a deficit equal to 16 percent of GDP by 2035 and would push federal debt to levels unprecedented in the United States. Debt would exceed 100 percent of GDP by 2023 and 200 percent by 2037.

The Long-Term Outlook for Spending

Excluding interest payments on debt held by the public, federal outlays have averaged 18.5 percent of GDP over the past 40 years. Such primary spending is now unusually high—and is expected to remain so through next year—because of the recent recession, tumult in financial markets, and policies implemented in response to those conditions. However, CBO projects that such outlays will decline to 20 percent of GDP by 2014.

Beyond that point, primary spending would rise again under both of CBO's long-term budget scenarios—to 24 percent of GDP by 2035 under the extended-baseline scenario and to 26 percent under the alternative fiscal scenario (see Table 1-2). In both cases, primary outlays would continue to grow steadily in later years.

Mandatory Outlays for Health Care Programs and Social Security

Federal spending for mandatory programs has grown sharply as a share of primary outlays in the past several decades, reaching about 60 percent in recent years. Most of that growth has been concentrated in the three largest entitlement programs—Medicare, Medicaid, and Social Security. Together, federal outlays for those three programs accounted for an average of 46 percent of primary spending over the past 10 years, up from 27 percent in 1975.

Table 1.2. Projected Spending and Revenues Under CBO's Long-Term Budget Scenarios.

(Percentage of gross domestic product)			
	2010	2020	2035
	Extended-Baseline Scenario		
Spending			
Primary spending			
Social Security	4.8	5.2	6.2
Medicare[a]	3.6	4.1	5.9
Medicaid, CHIP, and exchange subsidies	1.9	2.8	3.8
Other noninterest spending	12.5	8.3	7.8
Subtotal, primary spending	22.9	20.4	23.7
Interest spending	1.4	3.1	3.9
Total Spending	24.3	23.5	27.6
Revenues	14.9	20.7	23.3
Deficit (-) or Surplus			
Primary deficit or surplus	-8.0	0.3	-0.4
Total deficit	-9.4	-2.7	-4.3
Debt Held by the Public[b]	62	66	79

Table 1.2. (Continued)

(Percentage of gross domestic product)			
	2010	2020	2035
	Extended-Baseline Scenario		
	Alternative Fiscal Scenario		
Spending			
Primary spending			
Social Security	4.8	5.2	6.2
Medicare[a]	3.6	4.3	7.0
Medicaid, CHIP, and exchange subsidies	1.9	2.9	3.9
Other noninterest spending	12.5	9.7	9.3
Subtotal, primary spending	22.9	22.1	26.4
Interest spending	1.4	3.8	8.7
Total Spending	24.3	25.9	35.2
Revenues	14.9	19.3	19.3
Deficit			
Primary deficit	-8.0	-2.9	-7.2
Total deficit	-9.4	-6.6	-15.9
Debt Held by the Public[b]	62	87	185

Source: Congressional Budget Office.

Notes: Primary spending refers to all spending other than interest payments on federal debt. The primary deficit or surplus is the difference between revenues and primary spending.

The extended-baseline scenario adheres closely to current law, following CBO's 10-year baseline budget projections through 2020 (with adjustments for the recently enacted health care legislation) and then extending the baseline concept for the rest of the longterm projection period. The alternative fiscal scenario incorporates several changes to current law that are widely expected to occur or that would modify some provisions that might be difficult to sustain for a long period. (For details, see Table 1-1 on page 3.)

CHIP = Children's Health Insurance Program.

[a] Spending for Medicare beneficiaries includes amounts funded through beneficiaries' premiums.

[b] At the end of the year.

Under CBO's scenarios, all of the projected growth in primary outlays as a share of GDP in coming years stems from increases in mandatory spending, particularly in spending for the government's major health care programs: Medicare, Medicaid, the Children's Health Insurance Program (CHIP), and insurance subsidies that will be provided through the exchanges created by the recently enacted health care legislation. Under both of CBO's scenarios, total outlays for those health programs would roughly double as a share of GDP over the next 25 years, from 5.5 percent in 2010 to about 10 percent or 11 percent in 2035.[9] (For details about long-term projections of health care spending, see Chapter 2.) Spending on Social Security would rise much more slowly, from almost 5 percent of GDP in 2009 to about 6 percent in the 2030s and beyond (see Chapter 3).

Causes of Spending Growth

Two factors account for the projected increases in outlays for the government's large entitlement programs: the aging of the population and the rapid growth of health care costs per capita. The retirement of the large baby-boom generation born between 1946 and 1964 portends a long-lasting shift in the age profile of the U.S. population. That shift will substantially alter the balance between the working-age and retirement-age segments of the population. The share of people age 65 or older is projected to grow from 13 percent in 2010 to 20 percent in 2035, while the share of people ages 20 to 64 is expected to fall from 60 percent to 55 percent. In later decades, the aging of the population is expected to continue, but at a slower rate, because of increases in life expectancy.

In the case of Social Security, population aging drives the projected growth of spending as a percentage of GDP. Initial Social Security benefits are based on an individual's earnings, indexed to the overall growth of wages. Because average benefits increase at approximately the same rate as average earnings, economic growth does not significantly change Social Security spending as a share of GDP. How-ever, CBO projects that the number of workers per beneficiary will decline significantly over the next quarter century (from 2.9 in 2010 to 2.0 in 2035) and then will continue to drift downward.

In the case of the major mandatory health care programs, both aging and the rapid growth of per capita health care costs are responsible for the projected rise in federal spending as a share of GDP, because more elderly people will use increasingly expensive health care. (For a detailed breakdown of the roles played by those two factors, see Box 1-2 on page 10.) In its long-term projections, CBO anticipates that spending growth for health programs will moderate from past rates even if federal laws do not change (see Chapter 2). Both Medicaid and CHIP are financed jointly by the federal government and state governments, so growth in federal spending is expected to slow as states move to limit their costs. And even without changes to the laws governing Medicare, growth in spending on that program is projected to slow (though to a lesser degree than for the other health programs) because of future regulatory changes to the program and changes to the health care system as a whole.

Effects of Recent Legislation

The health care legislation enacted in March 2010—the Patient Protection and Affordable Care Act (P.L. 111-148), as modified by the Health Care and Education Reconciliation Act (P.L. 111- 152)—will cause major changes in the components of federal spending on health care. Both the expansion of eligibility for Medicaid and the provision of subsidies through new insurance exchanges will increase federal spending. At the same time, the legislation contains various provisions that will substantially reduce spending on Medicare relative to what would have occurred under prior law. On net, the legislation will raise federal spending on health care during most of the next two decades but lower it by the end of the second decade, according to the projections of CBO and the staff of the Joint Committee on Taxation (JCT). During that period, the net effects in either direction represent less than 0.5 percent of GDP in any year.

As discussed in Chapter 2, CBO does not believe it has an analytic basis for evaluating the effects of the legislation on the growth rate of spending over the very long run. Therefore, after the next decade or two (depending on the scenario), the projections in this chapter extrapolate federal spending on health care (including the incremental effects of the legislation) using the same growth rates that would be assumed in the absence of the legislation. Because those growth rates are applied to different levels of spending, however, health care spending varies from the amounts that would be projected without that legislation for the rest of the long-term projection period.

Differences Between the Long-Term Scenarios

Spending for Social Security would be identical under CBO's extended-baseline and alternative fiscal scenarios, and spending for Medicaid, CHIP, and the exchange subsidies would be very similar. In the case of Medicare, however, spending would be about 1 percentage point higher relative to GDP in 2035 under the alternative fiscal scenario than under the extended-baseline scenario, and the difference would widen to 2 percentage points by 2080. Those projected spending paths differ for two main reasons:

Box 1-2. How the Aging of the Population and Rising Costs for Health Care Affect Federal Spending on Major Mandatory Programs

In the Congressional Budget Office's (CBO's) longterm projections of spending, growth in noninterest spending as a share of gross domestic product (GDP) is attributable entirely to increases in spending on several large mandatory programs: Social Security, Medicare, Medicaid, and (to a lesser extent) insurance subsidies that will be provided through the exchanges established by the recently enacted health care legislation.[1] The health programs are the main drivers of that growth; they are responsible for 80 percent of the total projected rise in spending on those mandatory programs over the next 25 years.

Two factors underlie the projected increase in federal spending on the government's major mandatory health care programs and Social Security: the aging of the U.S. population, which increases the number of beneficiaries in those programs, and rapid growth in health care costs per beneficiary. CBO calculated how much of the projected rise in federal spending for the health care programs and Social Security under the extended-baseline scenario is attributable to aging and how much is attributable to "excess cost growth"—the extent to which health care costs per enrollee (adjusted for changes in the age profile of the population) grow faster than GDP per capita. CBO made that calculation by comparing the outlays projected under the extended-baseline scenario with the outlays that would occur under two alternative paths: one with an aging population but no excess cost growth for health care programs, and one with no aging but with excess cost growth.

The interaction between the aging of the population and excess cost growth accentuates their individual effects. As aging causes the number of beneficiaries of Medicare and Medicaid to rise, higher health care spending per person has a larger impact. Conversely, when health care costs are growing, having more beneficiaries imposes a larger budgetary cost. That interaction can be identified separately, or—as in CBO's analysis—it can be allocated according to the shares attributable to aging and excess cost growth.

Of the two factors, aging is the more important over the next 25 years. With the interaction allocated between the two, aging accounts for 63 percent of the total projected growth in spending on Social Security and the major mandatory health care programs by 2035, and excess cost growth accounts for 37 percent (see the table above and the figure at right). That result is not surprising given that the aging of the baby-boom generation will significantly expand the number of people participating in many of those programs.

Over the longer term, however, the situation changes. By 2080, excess cost growth is responsible for 56 percent of the total projected growth in federal spending on the health care programs and Social Security, and the share attributable to aging falls to 44 percent. The impact of excess cost growth is felt only in the health care programs; rising health care costs have no direct effect on spending for Social Security. Given the substantial uncertainties that exist about long-term rates of cost growth for health care, much more caution should be applied to those longer-term projections. (For a discussion of the rates of excess cost growth that underlie those calculations, and the basis for them, see Chapter 2.)

Explaining Projected Growth in Federal Spending on Major Mandatory Health Care Programs and Social Security by 2035 and 2080, by Source

Percent)		
	Aging	Excess Cost Growth
	Major Health Care Programs and Social Security	
2035	63	37
2080	44	56
	Major Health Care Programs	
2035	45	55
2080	29	71

Source: Congressional Budget Office.

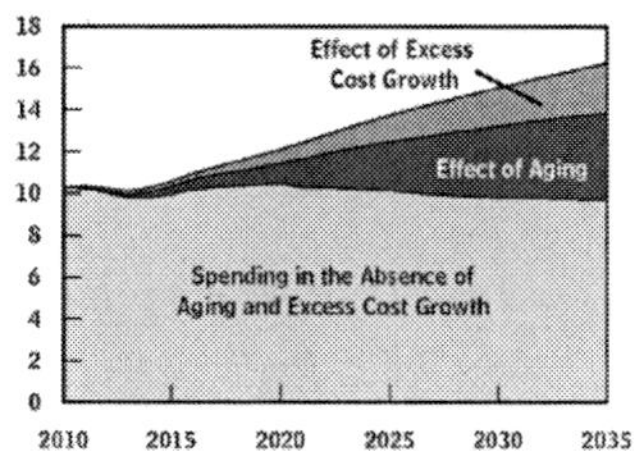

Source: Congressional Budget Office.

Sources of Growth in Federal Spending on Major Mandatory Health Care Programs and Social Security, 2010 to 2035

Looking only at the major health care programs, CBO found excess cost growth to be the main factor responsible for the projected increase in federal spending for those programs. Specifically, excess cost growth accounts for 55 percent of the programs' projected growth by 2035 and 71 percent by 2080. Again, the precision of those calculations should not be taken as an indication of certainty. Future rates of aging and especially of excess cost growth could differ substantially from CB O's assumptions, particularly in the longer term.

[1] Under the new law, certain people with income up to 400 percent of the federal poverty level will be eligible for federal subsidies to reduce their cost of obtaining private health insurance coverage. Although the premium subsidies are structured as tax credits, most of the funds involved will be classified as outlays because their value will generally exceed what recipients' income tax liability would otherwise be. CBO's spending projections for major mandatory health care programs also include the Children's Health Insurance Program, but spending on that program constitutes less than 0.1 percent of GDP.

- Under the current-law assumptions of the extended- baseline scenario, Medicare's sustainable growth rate mechanism would reduce payment rates for physicians by 21 percent this year, with additional smaller reductions for the next few years.[10] Under the alternative fiscal scenario, by contrast, Medicare's payment rates for physicians would be stable in 2010 and then increase gradually.
- The extended-baseline scenario incorporates the effects of the recent health care legislation, as estimated by CBO and JCT, over the next 20 years and then extrapolates those effects on spending levels in later years.[11] By contrast, the alternative fiscal scenario incorporates the estimated effects of that legislation for only 10 years and then extrapolates the estimated changes in spending levels beyond that. In particular, several policies that would restrain the growth of spending for Medicare are assumed in the alternative scenario not to be in effect after 2020, yielding a higher level of spending in the 2020s and beyond.

The upshot of those differences is that Medicare spending in 2035 is projected to be about 17 percent higher under the alternative fiscal scenario than under the extended-baseline scenario—a difference that persists in later years because the growth rates of spending beyond that point are the same under the two scenarios. That gap highlights the important implications of those health care policies for the federal budget.

Under both scenarios, the trust funds for Social Security and Part A of Medicare would become insolvent during the long-term projection period.[12] However, to measure the imbalance between the revenues and the outlays for benefits currently specified in law, CBO assumed that the two programs would continue to pay benefits as now scheduled. (Spending for other parts of Medicare also flows through a trust fund, but automatic infusions of general funds effectively ensure that it cannot become insolvent. Medicaid has no underlying trust fund.)

Other Federal Outlays

A larger difference between the two scenarios involves projections of federal spending for everything besides the major mandatory health programs and Social Security. Other primary spending (net of Medicare premiums and other offsetting receipts) would total about 8 percent of GDP in 2020 under the extended-baseline scenario and about 10 percent under the alternative fiscal scenario, declining slowly thereafter in both cases. Under the extended-baseline scenario, interest payments by the government would increase to almost 4 percent of GDP by 2035 and then remain close to that level thereafter. Under the alternative fiscal scenario, interest spending would equal 9 percent of GDP in 2035 and would continue to rise dramatically—by 2055, it would exceed that year's total federal revenues.

Other Noninterest Spending Under the Extended-Baseline Scenario

For the extended-baseline scenario, CBO used its 2010–2020 baseline projections of outlays for programs other than the major mandatory health care programs and Social Security. This year, about one- seventh of those outlays (or about 1.9 percent of GDP) are associated with the federal government's response to the recent recession.[13] Over the coming decade, such spending is either scheduled to expire under current law or is explicitly assumed in CBO's projections to be temporary and not to recur. Much of the rest of the government's other noninterest spending—including spending on military operations in Iraq and Afghanistan (which is expected to equal 1.1 percent of GDP this year)—is assumed to increase at the same rate as inflation through 2020. Because output generally grows faster than prices do, that spending is projected to shrink as a share of GDP: from 12.5 percent this year to 10.9 percent in 2012 and 8.3 percent in 2020.

For later years, other noninterest outlays are generally assumed to remain constant at their 2020 levels as a share of GDP under the extended-baseline scenario. However, two components of that spending were modeled explicitly.

First, premiums paid by Medicare beneficiaries and certain payments by states to Medicare—which are classified as offsetting receipts (that is, as offsets to outlays) and which will equal 0.4 percent of GDP in 2010—are projected to increase at the same rate as gross Medicare outlays.[14] When those offsetting receipts rise, total spending falls. Second, the refundable portions of the earned income tax credit and the child tax credit, which the budget records as outlays, were modeled along with revenues. Such refunds are projected to decrease over time as incomes rise. Because of the projected changes in those two components, other primary spending is projected to decline to 7.8 percent of GDP by 2035. For comparison, over the past 40 years, such spending has never fallen below 8.3 percent of GDP.

Other Noninterest Spending Under the Alternative Fiscal Scenario

In the alternative fiscal scenario, spending for most programs other than the major mandatory health care programs and Social Security is assumed to match CBO's baseline projections for the next few years (12.5 percent of GDP in 2010, 12.4 percent in 2011, and 10.9 percent in 2012). For subsequent years, CB O's starting point was to assume that such spending would remain at this year's levels relative to GDP rather than declining to the 2020 levels relative to GDP projected in the baseline. However, in extrapolating this year's levels, CBO removed the budgetary effect of unusual, short- term policies related to current economic conditions. With those policies (and offsetting receipts related to Medicare) excluded, primary spending on programs other than the major mandatory health care programs and Social Security will equal 10.5 percent of GDP in 2010, CBO estimates. Under the alternative fiscal scenario, that percentage would continue from 2013 through the end of the long-term projection period.

Net of offsetting receipts from Medicare and outlays on refundable tax credits, other noninterest spending is projected to equal 10.2 percent of GDP in 2013. Thereafter, because of increases in offsetting receipts and decreases in tax credit refunds, the net amount is projected to decline to 9.3 percent of GDP by 2035.

Interest Spending

For much of the past decade, federal debt was relatively constant as a share of GDP, but federal interest spending declined (from 2.3 percent of GDP in 2000 to 1.3 percent in 2009) because interest rates fell. In its 10-year baseline projections, CBO projects that interest spending will increase again—

to 2.0 percent of GDP in 2013 and 3.1 percent in 2020—as federal debt grows and interest rates rebound from their recent unusually low levels.

For the long-term budget projections, CBO assumed that interest rates would remain stable after 2020, meaning that interest outlays would grow at the same pace as federal debt. Under the extended-baseline scenario, annual interest spending would approach 4 percent of GDP by 2035 and then grow slowly, reaching 5 percent in 2080. Under the alternative fiscal scenario, interest spending would grow much faster—from 4 percent of GDP in 2020 to almost 9 percent by 2035 and much more in later years—because of widening deficits and ballooning debt. As discussed later in this chapter, higher federal debt would in fact lead to higher interest rates, making interest outlays even larger, particularly under the alternative fiscal scenario.

The Long-Term Outlook for Revenues

Federal revenues have fluctuated between 15 percent and 21 percent of GDP over the past 40 years, averaging about 18 percent. Just as spending priorities have changed during that period, the composition of revenues has shifted. Receipts from payroll taxes have grown faster than GDP, producing a larger share of total revenue.[15] At the same time, the shares of revenue contributed by corporate income taxes and excise taxes have shrunk.

After totaling nearly 18 percent of GDP in 2008, federal revenues fell sharply the following year, to about 15 percent of GDP, because of the recession and the tax cuts enacted in response to it. CBO expects revenues to remain near 15 percent of GDP this year. However, under the current-law assumptions of CBO's baseline, revenues would rebound over the next decade with improvement in the economy, the scheduled expiration of tax cuts enacted in 2001 and 2003, and sharp growth in the number of taxpayers subject to the alternative minimum tax. As a result, revenues would equal 19 percent of GDP in 2012 and close to 21 percent in 2020.

Under the extended-baseline scenario, revenues would continue to rise gradually thereafter, reaching 23 percent of GDP by 2035. That increase would occur largely because, under current law, real growth in income would push people into higher tax brackets over time and inflation-related increases in income would make more income subject to the AMT. As a result of those factors, the effective marginal tax rate on labor income would rise from 29 percent today to about 38 percent in 2035. Revenues would also increase relative to GDP throughout the projection period because the recently enacted excise tax on certain high-premium health insurance plans would affect a growing share of plans over time. All told, average tax rates (taxes as a share of income) would rise considerably, and people at various points in the income scale would pay a very different percentage of their income in taxes than people at the same points do today.

For the alternative fiscal scenario, by contrast, CBO assumed that current tax law would be changed over time to continue certain policies to which people have grown accustomed and to keep revenues as a percentage of GDP more consistent with past patterns. Specifically, CBO assumed that through 2020, most of the tax cuts enacted in 2001 and 2003 would continue (except rate reductions applying to high-income taxpayers), relief from the AMT would continue, and the estate tax would be extended with the rates and exemption amounts (adjusted for inflation) in effect in 2009. (If those changes to current law were made, they would receive special treatment under the Statutory Pay-As-You-Go Act of 2010, as explained in Box 1-1 on page 4.) Beyond 2020, CBO assumed that tax law would evolve to keep total revenues at the same share of GDP as in 2020. Under those assumptions, revenues would increase to just over 19 percent of GDP in 2020 (rather than the almost 21 percent under the extended-baseline scenario) and would remain at that level in later years. Thus, revenues projected under the alternative fiscal scenario are lower than those estimated under the extended-baseline scenario by more than 1 percent of GDP in 2020 and by about 4 percent in 2035. (Details of CBO's long-term revenue projections are presented in Chapter 4.)

The Size of the Fiscal Imbalance

How large is the long-term budgetary shortfall facing the U.S. government? Two measures offer complementary perspectives: Annual amounts of federal debt show how shortfalls accumulate over time, whereas the "fiscal gap" summarizes the shortfall over a given period in a single value. Both measures show that projected revenues are insufficient to support projected spending—with a fairly modest divergence under the extended-baseline scenario and a very large one under the alternative fiscal scenario. Looking at how the fiscal gap changes over time demonstrates the effect of delaying action to address the budgetary imbalance.

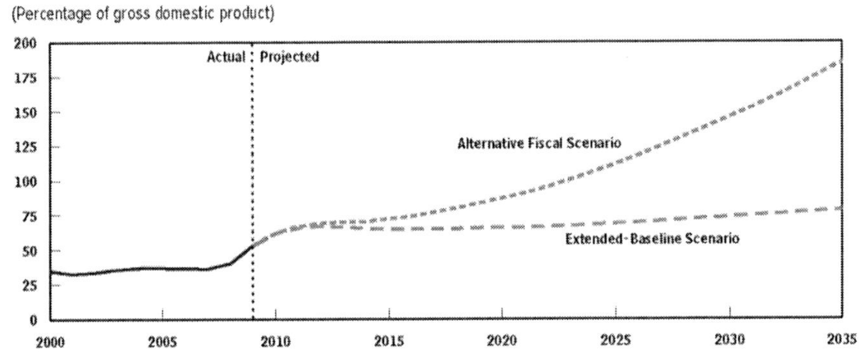

Source: Congressional Budget Office.

Note: The extended-baseline scenario adheres closely to current law, following CBO's 10-year baseline budget projections through 2020 (with adjustments for the recently enacted health care legislation) and then extending the baseline concept for the rest of the longterm projection period. The alternative fiscal scenario incorporates several changes to current law that are widely expected to occur or that would modify some provisions that might be difficult to sustain for a long period. (For details, see Table 1-1 on page 3.)

Figure 1.2. Federal Debt Held by the Public Under CBO's Long-Term Budget Scenarios.

The Accumulation of Federal Debt

For a combination of federal spending and revenues to be sustainable over time, the resulting debt must eventually grow no faster than the economy. The most meaningful measure of federal debt for such projections is debt held by the public, which represents the amount that the government is borrowing in the financial markets (by issuing Treasury securities) to pay for federal operations and activities. That borrowing competes with other participants in the credit markets for financial resources and can crowd out private investment.[16]

A useful barometer of fiscal policy is the amount of government debt held by the public relative to annual economic output. Such debt stood at 40 percent of GDP at the end of 2008, a little above the 40-year average of 36 percent. Since then, large deficits have caused debt held by the public to increase sharply—to 53 percent of GDP at the end of 2009 and, CBO projects, to 62 percent by the end of this year. Debt has exceeded 50 percent of GDP during only one other period in U.S. history: between 1942 and 1956, when it spiked (peaking at 109 percent of GDP) because of a surge in federal spending during World War II.

Under the assumptions of CBO's extended-baseline scenario, annual budget deficits would decline to 2.3 percent of GDP by 2014. After that, both deficits and debt would remain stable relative to GDP for several years. But then growth in spending on the major mandatory health care programs, Social Security, and interest payments would cause deficits to increase, and debt would once again grow faster than the economy. By 2035, it would equal 79 percent of GDP (see Figure 1-2).

Under the alternative fiscal scenario, deficits would also decline for a few years after 2010 and then grow again, but at a much faster rate. By 2020, debt would approach 90 percent of GDP. After that, the growing imbalance between revenues and noninterest spending, combined with the spiraling cost of interest payments, would swiftly push debt to unsustainable levels. Debt would surpass its historical peak of 109 percent of GDP by 2025 and would exceed 200 percent of GDP in 2037.

The federal government could not issue ever-larger amounts of debt relative to the size of the economy indefinitely. If debt continued to rise rapidly relative to GDP, investors at some point would begin to doubt the government's willingness to pay interest on that debt. Therefore, under the alternative fiscal scenario, the government would eventually need to cut spending well below the levels projected under that scenario or increase taxes well above their average historical percentage of GDP to put the federal budget on a sustainable path.

Debt would rise much more slowly relative to GDP under the extended-baseline scenario because current law would lead to both of those sorts of adjustments. In that scenario, revenues would reach historically high levels (23.3 percent of GDP in 2035, compared with 19.3 percent under the alternative fiscal scenario), and noninterest spending for things other than the major mandatory health programs and Social Security would reach the lowest levels relative to output since before World War II (7.8 percent of GDP in 2035, compared with 9.3 percent under the alternative fiscal scenario). With the changes assumed in the extended-baseline scenario, the sharp increase in outlays projected for the major health care programs and Social Security could be accommodated with a fairly small increase in debt relative to the size of the economy.

Many budget analysts believe that the alternative fiscal scenario presents a more realistic picture of the nation's underlying fiscal policy than the extended-baseline scenario does—because, for example, it does not allow the impact of the AMT to expand substantially. The explosive path of federal debt under the alternative fiscal scenario underscores the need for large and rapid policy changes to put the nation on a sustainable fiscal course.

Table 1.3. The Federal Fiscal Gap Under CBO's Long-Term Budget Scenarios.

Present Value of the Future Stream of Revenues or Outlays over a Given Period			
Projection Period	Revenues or Outlays over a Given Period Present Value of the Future Stream of		Fiscal Gap (Outlays minus revenues)
	Revenues	Outlays	
	Extended-Baseline Scenario		
25 Years (2010 to 2034)	22.7	23.9	1.2
50 Years (2010 to 2059)	23.7	24.5	0.8
75 Years (2010 to 2084)	25.0	25.7	0.7
	Alternative Fiscal Scenario		
25 Years (2010 to 2034)	20.7	25.5	4.8
50 Years (2010 to 2059)	19.8	26.7	6.9
75 Years (2010 to 2084)	19.5	28.2	8.7

Source: Congressional Budget Office.

Notes: The fiscal gap is a measure of federal shortfalls over a given period. It represents the extent to which the government would need to immediately and permanently either raise tax revenues or cut spending—or do both, to some degree—to make the government's debt the same size (relative to gross domestic product, or GDP) at the end of the period that it was at the beginning of 2010.

To allow for the increase in the nominal value of federal debt that would occur even if that debt was maintained at its current share of GDP, outlays include current debt, and revenues include the present value of the target end-of-period debt. (The end-of-period debt is equal to GDP in the last year of the period multiplied by the ratio of debt to GDP at the beginning of 2010. A present value is a single number that describes a flow of future revenues or outlays in terms of an equivalent lump sum received or spent today.)

The extended-baseline scenario adheres closely to current law, following CBO's 10-year baseline budget projections through 2020 (with adjustments for the recently enacted health care legislation) and then extending the baseline concept for the rest of the longterm projection period. The alternative fiscal scenario incorporates several changes to current law that are widely expected to occur or that modify some current provisions that might be difficult to sustain for a long period. (For details, see Table 1-1 on page 3.)

The Fiscal Gap

How much would policies have to change to avoid unsustainable increases in government debt? A useful answer comes from looking at the fiscal gap, which measures the immediate change in spending or revenues that would be necessary to keep the debt-to-GDP ratio the same at the end of a given period as at the beginning of the period. The fiscal gap is conceptually similar to the actuarial imbalance for Social Security (see Table 3-1 in Chapter 3). Both measures quantify a long-term shortfall in present-value terms—that is, as a single number that describes a flow of future revenues or outlays in terms of an equivalent lump sum received or spent today—and both can be expressed as a share of GDP.[17]

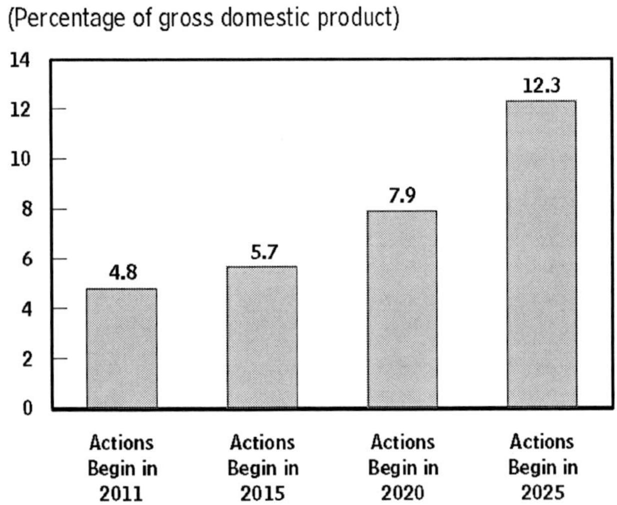

Source: Congressional Budget Office.

Notes: Primary spending refers to all spending other than interest payments on federal debt.

The fiscal gap is a measure of federal shortfalls over a given period. It represents the extent to which the government would need to immediately and permanently either raise tax revenues or cut spending—or do both, to some degree—to make the government's debt the same size (relative to gross domestic product) at the end of the period that it was at the beginning of 2010.

The alternative fiscal scenario incorporates several changes to current law that are widely expected to occur or that would modify some provisions that might be difficult to sustain for a long period. (For details, see Table 1-1 on page 3.)

Figure 1.3. Reductions in Primary Spending or Increases in Revenues in Various Years Needed to Close the 25-Year Fiscal Gap Under CBO's Alternative Fiscal Scenario.

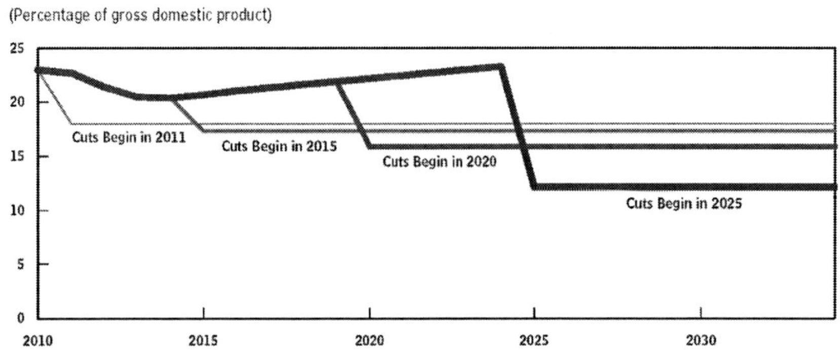

Source: Congressional Budget Office.

Notes: Primary spending refers to all spending other than interest payments on federal debt.

Closing the 25-year fiscal gap would make federal debt the same size (relative to gross domestic product, or GDP) at the end of the period that it was at the beginning. This analysis uses the fiscal gap and revenue projections in CBO's alternative fiscal scenario and then calculates the amount of primary spending that would close the fiscal gap if spending was held constant as a share of GDP going forward from various points in time.

The alternative fiscal scenario incorporates several changes to current law that are widely expected to occur or that would modify some provisions that might be difficult to sustain for a long period. (For details, see Table 1-1 on page 3.)

Figure 1.4. Various Paths for Primary Spending That Would Close the 25-Year Fiscal Gap Under CBO's Alternative Fiscal Scenario.

The fiscal gap over the next 25 years would amount to 1.2 percent of GDP under the extended-baseline scenario or 4.8 percent under the alternative fiscal scenario (see Table 1-3). In other words, relative to the projections of the alternative fiscal scenario, an immediate and permanent reduction in spending or increase in revenues equal to 4.8 percent of GDP—the equivalent of almost $700 billion in this year's federal budget—would be needed to create a sustainable fiscal path for the next quarter century. If the change came entirely from revenues, it would amount to roughly a one-quarter increase in revenues relative to the amount projected for 2020 and later years. If the change came entirely from spending, it would represent a cut of roughly one-fifth in primary spending from the amount projected for 2020 and a cut of one-sixth from the amount projected for 2035.

Over 75 years, the fiscal gap would amount to only 0.7 percent of GDP under the extended-baseline scenario because revenues would be approximately the same as primary spending in the long term (though both would be much greater relative to GDP than in the past). Under the alternative fiscal scenario, deficits would grow every year, so the fiscal gap would be larger over longer periods. Creating a sustainable fiscal path for the next 75 years under that scenario would require immediate and permanent policy changes equal to 8.7 percent of GDP.

The Effect of Delaying Action on the Fiscal Imbalance

Waiting to close the fiscal gap would make the necessary changes larger. To illustrate the costs of delay, CBO simulated the effects of closing the fiscal gap under the alternative fiscal scenario beginning in 2011, 2015, 2020, or 2025. Those simulations indicate that postponing action would substantially increase the size of the policy adjustments needed to put the budget on a sustainable course. For example, if lawmakers wanted to close the fiscal gap through 2035 but did not begin until 2015, they would have to reduce primary spending or increase revenues over that period by 5.7 percent of GDP, rather than by 4.8 percent if they acted in 2011 (see Figure 1-3). If they waited until 2020 to close the fiscal gap through 2035, they would have to cut noninterest outlays or raise revenues over that period by 7.9 percent of GDP. Moreover, those simulations omit the effects that deficits and debt would have on economic growth and interest rates in the intervening years; incorporating such effects would make the impact of delaying policy changes even more severe.

Another perspective on the effects of delay comes from the so-called sustainable spending level—the fixed amount of outlays (measured as a share of GDP) that could be supported by a projected stream of revenues. To eliminate the fiscal gap through 2035 under the alternative fiscal scenario, primary outlays could be reduced to 17.3 percent of GDP in 2015 and later. If no changes were made until 2020, primary outlays would have to fall permanently to 15.9 percent of GDP, and if action was delayed until 2025, the projected revenue stream would only support primary outlays of 12.1 percent of GDP (see Figure 1-4). By comparison, primary outlays are expected to equal 23.0 percent of GDP this year.

Uncertainty of Long-Term Budget Projections

Future budgetary outcomes will depend in large part on future policies—as evidenced by the difference between the debt paths of the two scenarios analyzed in this chapter. But outcomes will also depend on factors outside the direct control of policymakers, such as the state of the economy and demographic trends. For example, if longterm economic growth is slower than projected, deficits will be greater for any given set of policies. Conversely, if fertility rates are higher than assumed or improvements in mortality are smaller, the population will be younger than projected, and spending on Social Security and Medicare will be lower as a percentage of GDP for any given set of policies. (Values for the major demographic and economic variables that underpin CBO's long-term projections are described in Appendix B.)

The government's future mandatory spending will also depend crucially on future health care costs. The rate at which health care costs have grown has varied greatly in the past. For an analysis of how altering CBO's assumptions about such cost growth would affect projected health care spending, see Chapter 2.

Although the size of future budgetary shortfalls is uncertain, if revenues remain at past levels relative to GDP—as under the alternative fiscal scenario—federal debt is likely to keep growing rapidly under any plausible assumptions about future trends in the economy, demographics, and health care costs. (For instance, if the rate of productivity growth was 50 percent higher than assumed in this chapter, or about equal to the rate seen during the 1960s, debt would still grow to more than 150 percent of GDP in 2035 under the alternative fiscal scenario.) And even if revenues increase significantly relative to GDP in the future—as under the extended-baseline scenario—debt is likely to remain at levels that are extremely high by past standards. Indeed, debt is already at historically high levels, and federal interest costs are likely to grow substantially when interest rates return to more normal levels.

The Economic Impact of Rising Federal Debt

The economic effects of growth in federal debt depend partly on the economic conditions that prevail when deficits are incurred. When the long-term outlook for the budget appears sustainable, running deficits for a limited time is not necessarily detrimental to the economy. Indeed, when the economy has substantial unemployment and unused factories, offices, and equipment, running deficits generally increases output and employment relative to what would occur with a balanced budget. For instance, the larger deficits that result from automatic declines in tax revenues or increases in government spending (such as for unemployment benefits) during and immediately after a recession help reduce the severity of the downturn by offsetting some of the decline in disposable income and thus supporting demand for goods and services.[18]

Similarly, policymakers' actions to go beyond such "automatic stabilizers" by reducing taxes and increasing spending further during a period of economic weakness can also lessen the severity of the downturn. As an example, CBO estimated that the spending increases and tax cuts enacted in the American Recovery and Reinvestment Act of 2009 (P.L. 111-5) boosted output and employment significantly during the past year compared with what would have happened in the absence of that legislation.[19] Thus, the federal government's ability to run budget deficits enables fiscal policy to offset some of the negative effects of recessions.

Even temporary deficits, however, produce increases in debt that have harmful consequences in the long run (assuming the government does not run budget surpluses later to retire the additional debt). Moreover, economic fluctuations resulting from business cycles are not the fundamental source of the long-term budgetary pressures facing the nation. Instead, outlays are projected to rise above the amount that can be funded from current rates of taxation because of increases in Social Security spending and, more important, continuing growth in federal spending on health care programs as a share of GDP (see Box 1-2 on page 10). If those developments are not prevented or offset through changes elsewhere in the budget, the resulting increase in deficits will hurt the economy through several channels, as described below.

At the same time, steps taken to address the looming deficits could also have negative consequences. Raising revenues significantly relative to GDP (as under the extended-baseline scenario) would harm the economy through the impact on people's decisions about how much to work and save. The size of that impact, and its implications for individuals, would depend crucially on the specific tax policies involved. Cutting federal spending could also have negative effects on individuals, businesses, and the economy.

Whatever policies lawmakers chose to tackle the fiscal imbalance, taking those actions earlier would lead to higher output in the long run, enhance the well-being of future generations, and reduce the risk of a fiscal crisis. At the same time, however, early action could make current generations worse off than if action was deferred.

Crowding Out of Capital and Related Economic Effects

Increased government borrowing tends to crowd out private investment in productive capital, leading to a smaller capital stock and lower output in the long run than would otherwise be the case. Deficits tend to have that effect on private investment because the portion of people's savings used to buy government bonds is not available to pay for such investment.

An exception is that government borrowing to finance public investment, such as improvements in infrastructure, need not reduce future output if the public investment is as productive as private investment. However, the long-term rise in debt projected by CBO is driven by increases in government transfer payments (such as spending on entitlement programs) rather than increases in government investment.

Other factors can offset some of that crowding-out effect. Greater government borrowing tends to lead to greater private saving, which increases the funds available both to purchase government debt and to finance private investment. Government borrowing generally boosts private saving for several reasons:

- Crowding out usually leads to higher interest rates, which raise the return on saving;
- Some people save more because they anticipate that taxes will be raised, or spending cut, in the future to cover the cost of paying interest on the accumulated debt; and
- The policies that give rise to deficits (such as tax cuts or increased government transfer payments) put more money in private hands, some of which is probably saved.

Overall, however, the offsetting rise in private saving is generally smaller than the change in the deficit, so greater government borrowing leads to lower national saving.

Lower national saving means that the nation as a whole is setting aside fewer resources for the future, which results in lower income in the long run than would otherwise occur. That reduction in saving leads to lower domestic investment. At the same time, however, higher interest rates attract more foreign capital to the United States and induce U.S. savers to keep more of their money at home. Such net inflows of capital prevent U.S. investment from declining as much as national saving does.[20] But those capital inflows also create the obligation for more profits and interest to flow overseas in the future. Therefore, although flows of capital into the United States can help maintain domestic investment, most of the gains from that additional investment do not accrue to U.S. residents.

CBO has analyzed the economic effects of rising federal debt under two sets of assumptions. Those analyses go beyond the long-term budget projections, which assume a stable economy unaffected by deficits in the long run. (The stable economic conditions assumed by CBO include a constant real interest rate on federal debt after 2020 and steady growth rates for real wages and output after that year.)

In the first case, CBO assessed the impact on the economy if private saving and capital inflows from other countries were to respond to changes in deficits according to simple rules that reflect how they have behaved in the past.[21] Specifically, CBO assumed that for each $1 increase in the deficit, consumption would fall—and therefore, other things being equal, private saving would rise—by 40 cents. On net, those changes in government and private saving would cause national saving to fall by 60 cents. In addition, CBO assumed that capital inflows would increase by 24 cents (40 percent of the 60-cent change in national saving), leading domestic investment to decline, all else being equal, by 36 cents. The analysis also incorporated the channels through which crowding out reduces tax revenue (by reducing GDP) and raises net interest payments (by raising interest rates), thereby increasing federal borrowing further and causing additional crowding out.[22]

Because those assumptions are based largely on past outcomes, they serve as useful rules of thumb in situations that are within the range of experience. However, if interest rates and the debt-to-GDP ratio rise to levels rarely seen before, such rules of thumb may no longer apply.

CBO estimates that with those rules of thumb applied, real GDP per person under the alternative fiscal scenario would be about 6 percent lower in 2025 and 15 percent lower in 2035 than it would be under the stable economic conditions (with no crowding out) assumed for the long-term budget projections (see Figure 1-5). Those reductions would occur because of the crowding out of investment. Nevertheless, real GDP per person would still be considerably higher in 2025 and 2035 than it is now because of continued growth in productivity. Incorporating the lower output and higher interest rates implied by crowding out would accelerate the projected growth of debt as a percentage of GDP. As a result, under the alternative fiscal scenario, debt as a percentage of GDP would be substantially higher than it would be without accounting for crowding out (see Figure 1-6 on page 22).

Part of the growing budget deficits projected for coming years would be financed by capital inflows from other countries, so a rising portion of GDP would have to be sent abroad as profits or interest on those capital inflows and thus would not be available to U.S. households. For that reason, the effects of crowding out on GDP (which is equal to all income earned from productive activities in the United States) would be smaller than the effects on gross national product (GNP, which equals GDP plus income received from other countries minus income sent abroad).[23] Crowding out would reduce real GNP per person by 8 percent in 2025 and by 21 percent in 2035, CBO estimates (see Figure 1-5).

Deficits, and thus crowding-out effects, would be much smaller under the extended-baseline scenario. Projections like those discussed above (for the alternative fiscal scenario) show that real GDP per person and real GNP per person would both be slightly lower—and debt as a percentage of GDP slightly higher—under the extended- baseline scenario than under stable economic conditions. However, those projections of GDP, GNP, and debt do not incorporate the negative impact that the higher tax rates in effect under that scenario would have on incentives to work and save.

In the second case, CBO analyzed the effects of rising debt using a model of the economy that assumes that people make decisions about how much to work and save on the basis of current and anticipated government policies and economic conditions (such as wages and interest rates). In that analysis, CBO compared economic outcomes under a policy that would stabilize the ratio of debt to GDP earlier with outcomes under a policy that would allow that ratio to grow for another 10 years before being stabilized. The underlying budgetary assumptions used in the analysis follow those of the alternative fiscal scenario (adapted for that particular model) until policy is changed to stabilize the debt-to-GDP ratio.[24] In principle, that ratio could be stabilized through any number of government policies. CBO analyzed two possible policies: one in which marginal tax rates were increased, and one in which government transfer payments (which were assumed to go mainly to older people) were reduced.

CBO's analysis suggests that delaying action for 10 years—and thus allowing the debt-to-GDP ratio to rise by an additional 30 percentage points under the assumptions of the analysis—would cause output to be about 2 percent to 4 percent lower in the long run than it would be if the ratio was stabilized earlier at lower levels, depending on the policy used to stabilize the debt. (Despite those reductions, output would continue to be higher than current levels because of growth in productivity.) Most of the reduction in output would stem from two factors: the crowding out of investment in productive capital, which would cause the capital stock to be 6 percent to 10 percent smaller if action was delayed, and the effects of higher marginal tax rates on incentives to work and save (in the case of the policy involving higher taxes).

Another conclusion of CBO's analysis is that generations born after about 2015 would be worse off if action to stabilize the debt-to-GDP ratio was postponed from 2015 to 2025. People born before 1990, however, would be better off if action was delayed, largely because they would partly or wholly avoid the policy changes needed to stabilize the debt (leaving aside the negative effects of a possible fiscal crisis or of reduced flexibility for the government to respond to economic challenges, as described below). Finally, generations born between 1990 and 2015 could either gain or lose from a delay depending on the details of the policy used to stabilize the debt (again leaving aside some other effects of growing debt). In the long run, a 10-year delay would reduce the well-being of all future generations by amounts equivalent to a cut of roughly 1 percent to 2 percent of their lifetime consumption, depending on the specific policies adopted.

Other Consequences of Rising Federal Debt

Besides the outcomes described above, which would unfold incrementally over time, higher debt could raise the probability of a fiscal crisis in which investors would lose confidence in the government's willingness to fully honor its obligations, and thus, the government would be forced to pay much more for debt financing.[25] Interest rates might rise only gradually to reflect growing uncertainty about whether government debt would be fully honored, but other countries' experiences suggest that a loss of investor confidence could occur abruptly instead.

If interest rates on government debt spiked, the value of outstanding government debt would fall sharply. That decline in value could precipitate a broader financial crisis by causing large losses for mutual funds, pension funds, insurance companies, banks, and other holders of federal debt. Experience in other countries suggests that resolving such a crisis would require fiscal policy changes that would be far more drastic and painful than if policies had been adjusted sooner to avoid a crisis.

Higher debt would also reduce policymakers' ability to respond to unexpected challenges, such as economic downturns or international crises. Lower amounts of debt, by contrast, give the government the ability to borrow to meet sudden needs. If federal debt had been larger in 2008 than it was, the government might have had less flexibility to respond to the financial turmoil and slumping economy by using money to stimulate economic activity and stabilize the financial sector while continuing to fund its other commitments. Greater debt in the future would increase the risk that investors would be unwilling to finance all of the outlays or revenue reductions needed to deal with unforeseen events unless they were compensated with very high interest rates. Instead, to reassure investors concerned about a widening deficit during a recession, policymakers might be forced to raise taxes or reduce spending suddenly, probably exacerbating already weak economic conditions.

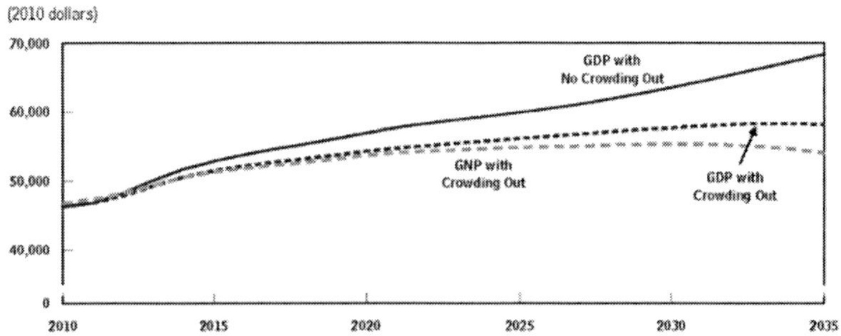

Source: Congressional Budget Office.

Notes: "Crowding out" refers to the fact that government borrowing (to finance deficits) tends to crowd out private investment in productive capital, leading to a smaller capital stock and lower output and income in the long run than would otherwise occur.

The alternative fiscal scenario incorporates several changes to current law that are widely expected to occur or that would modify some provisions that might be difficult to sustain for a long period. (For details, see Table 1-1 on page 3.)

The values for GNP with no crowding out (not shown here) are about the same as those for GDP with no crowding out.

GDP = gross domestic product; GNP = gross national product.

Figure 1.5. The Effects of Crowding Out on Real GDP and GNP per Person Under CBO's Alternative Fiscal Scenario.

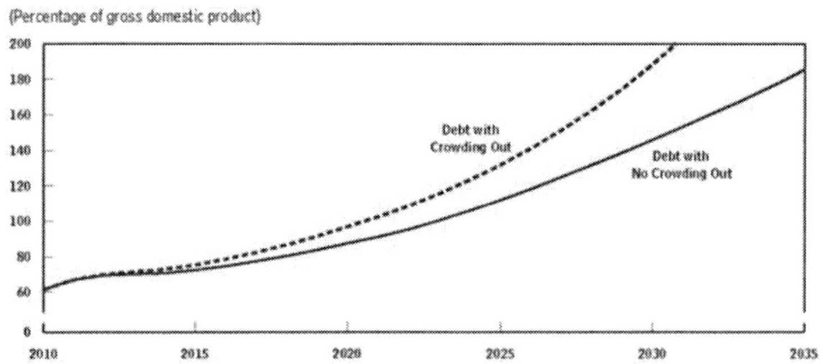

Source: Congressional Budget Office.

Notes: "Crowding out" refers to the fact that government borrowing (to finance deficits) tends to crowd out private investment in productive capital, leading to a smaller capital stock and lower output and income in the long run than would otherwise occur.

The alternative fiscal scenario incorporates several changes to current law that are widely expected to occur or that would modify some provisions that might be difficult to sustain for a long period. (For details, see Table 1-1 on page 3.)

Figure 1.6. The Effects of Crowding Out on Federal Debt Held by the Public Under CBO's Alternative Fiscal Scenario.

Even in the absence of a crisis, the longer that debt kept growing, the more significant would be the policy changes needed to control it, which could further increase the burden of fiscal tightening on future generations. Large and abrupt changes in fiscal policy, such as cuts in government transfer payments, would be more difficult for people to adjust to than smaller and more gradual changes. In addition, larger increases in tax rates would lead to greater losses in economic efficiency by reducing incentives for work and saving.

Changes in CBO's Long-Term Projections Since June 2009

The long-term paths for primary spending presented in this chapter are similar to the ones that CBO published last year, but the paths for revenues differ.[26] In the extended-baseline scenario, the recent enactment of major health care legislation has increased projected revenues, particularly in the 2030s and beyond, thus slowing the accumulation of debt considerably. In the alternative fiscal scenario, the health care legislation and changes in CBO's assumptions have pushed up projected revenues in the next few decades but lowered them thereafter. As in last year's projection for that scenario, debt accumulates very rapidly.

Changes in Projections Under the Extended-Baseline Scenario

Compared with the previous long-term outlook, CBO's current projections for primary spending under the extended-baseline scenario are slightly higher before 2020 and are a little lower after 2030 (see the top panel of Figure 1-7). The longer-run difference arises almost entirely because CBO has reduced its projection of spending on major mandatory health care programs for later years of the projection period. That reduction reflects two factors: technical changes in the projected growth rate of health care costs and a slightly lower projected level of health care spending in 2030 because of the recent legislation (see Chapter 2).

The largest change in the extended-baseline scenario since last year is a significant increase in projected revenues as a percentage of GDP, especially in the 2030s and later years. Whereas previously CBO projected that total revenues would reach 22 percent of GDP in 2035 and 26 percent in 2080, the current extended-baseline scenario has revenues growing to 23 percent of GDP in 2035 and 30 percent in 2080 (an increase of 4 percentage points for that year). Most of the change in revenues stems from the new excise tax on high-premium health insurance plans that is scheduled to take effect in 2018. That tax will not only generate additional revenues directly when it is paid but also increase revenues if people opt to avoid it by selecting lower-cost health insurance plans, thus resulting in a larger share of compensation taking the form of taxable wages. Combining all of the direct and indirect effects, CBO projects that the new excise tax will increase revenues as a share of GDP by just over half a percentage point in 2035 and by more than 3 percentage points in 2080.

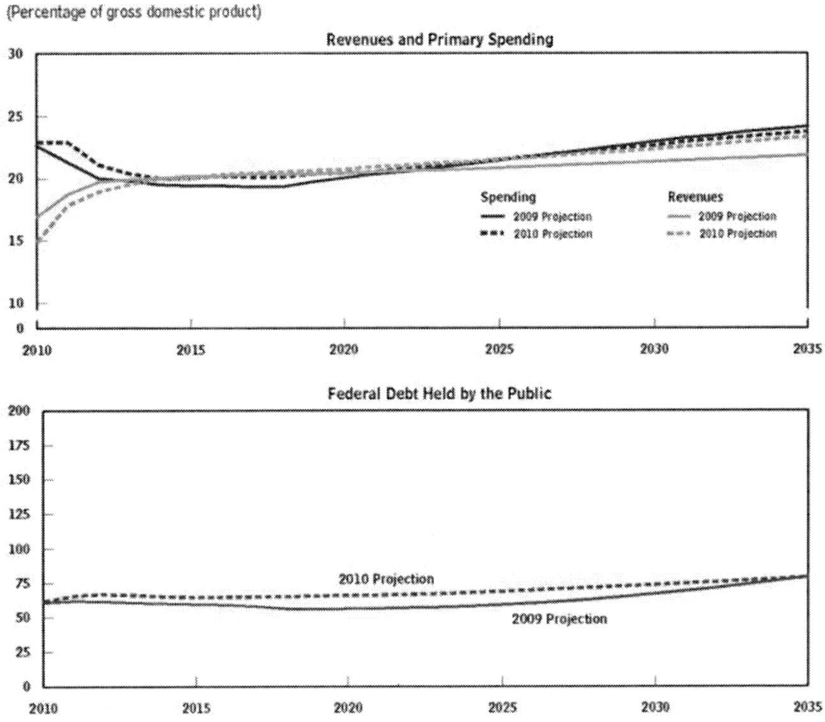

Source: Congressional Budget Office.

Notes: Primary spending refers to all spending other than interest payments on federal debt.

The extended-baseline scenario adheres closely to current law, following CBO's 10-year baseline budget projections through 2020 (with adjustments for the recently enacted health care legislation) and then extending the baseline concept for the rest of the longterm projection period. (For details, see Table 1-1 on page 3.)

Figure 1.7. Comparison of CBO's 2009 and 2010 Budget Projections Under the Extended-Baseline Scenario.

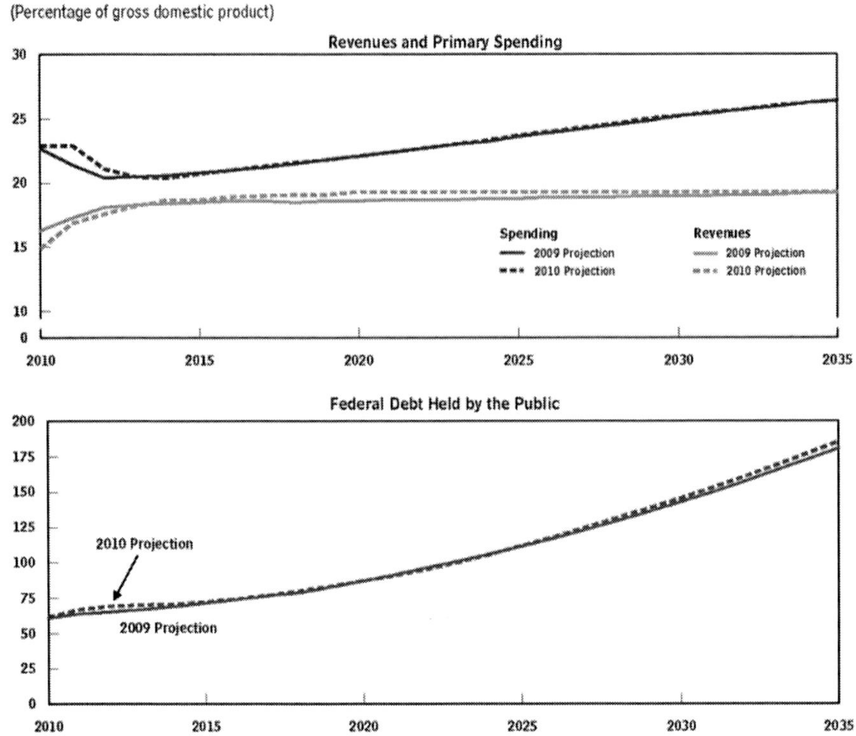

Source: Congressional Budget Office.

Notes: Primary spending refers to all spending other than interest payments on federal debt.

The alternative fiscal scenario incorporates several changes to current law that are widely expected to occur or that would modify some provisions that might be difficult to sustain for a long period. (For details, see Table 1-1 on page 3.)

Figure 1.8. Comparison of CBO's 2009 and 2010 Budget Projections Under the Alternative Fiscal Scenario.

Federal debt is slightly higher in the next few decades under the extended-baseline scenario than was projected in 2009 (see the bottom panel of Figure 1-7). In later decades, however, debt is substantially lower because of the higher projected growth in revenues. In the 2009 projection, revenues grew more slowly than outlays, and debt rose rapidly after 2030, reaching 200 percent of GDP in 2067. In the current projection, revenues and outlays follow similar paths throughout the long-term projection period. As a result, debt grows much less—from its current level of about 60 percent of GDP to 75 percent by 2032 and exceeding 100 percent by 2080.

Changes in Projections Under the Alternative Fiscal Scenario

The differences between CBO's current and previous projections of primary spending under the alternative fiscal scenario are very small. On average, outlays are 0.1 percent of GDP lower over the projection period (see the top panel of Figure 1-8), mostly because of changes in projected health care spending.

The revisions to revenues are slightly more complicated. CBO's 2009 projection was based on the assumption that receipts from income taxes would consistently grow faster than GDP, causing total projected revenues to gradually increase from 18 percent of GDP in 2012 to 19 percent in 2035 and 22 percent in 2080. In the current projection, revenues are estimated to rise at a faster rate over the next decade, primarily because of the economic recovery and the additional taxes imposed by the health care legislation. However, tax policy is assumed to adjust after 2020 so revenues remain at their projected 2020 level (just over 19 percent of GDP) for the rest of the longterm projection period. Consequently, revenues are projected to be higher for years before 2035 and lower afterward.

Taking those changes together, the striking increase in debt that was projected under the alternative fiscal scenario in last year's report is apparent this year as well (see the bottom panel of Figure 1-8). Federal debt is projected to reach 100 percent of GDP in 2023 and then continue to grow at an unsustainable pace.

2. The Long-Term Outlook for Mandatory Spending on Health Care

Spending for health care in the United States has been growing faster than the economy for many years, posing a challenge not only for the federal government's two major health insurance programs, Medicare and Medicaid, but also for state and local governments and the private sector. Measured as a percentage of the nation's gross domestic product, total spending on health care services and supplies increased from 5 percent in 1960 to 10 percent in 1985 and 15 percent in 2008, the most recent calendar year for which data are available. Federal spending for Medicare and Medicaid rose from 2.2 percent of GDP in fiscal year 1985 to 5.3 percent in 2009. Underlying those trends, health care spending per person has grown faster than the nation's economic output per person by an average of about 2 percentage points per year over long periods. Key factors contributing to that faster growth are the emergence and increased use of new medical technologies, rising personal income, and the expanding scope of health insurance coverage.

Such rates of growth cannot continue indefinitely, however, because if they did, total spending on health care would eventually account for all of the country's economic output—an implausible outcome. Instead, over time, people will try to limit their spending for health care in order to maintain their consumption of other goods and services. In addition, state governments—which pay a large share of Medicaid's costs and have considerable influence on those costs—will need to reduce spending growth in order to balance their budgets. Thus, even in the absence of changes in federal law, growth in spending on Medicaid and on health care in the private sector will gradually slow. The rate of growth of spending on Medicare is also expected to slow, but to a lesser extent, reflecting changes in medical practices common to all patients, regulatory changes allowed under the law, and the increasing pressure of premiums and cost-sharing requirements on enrollees' finances.

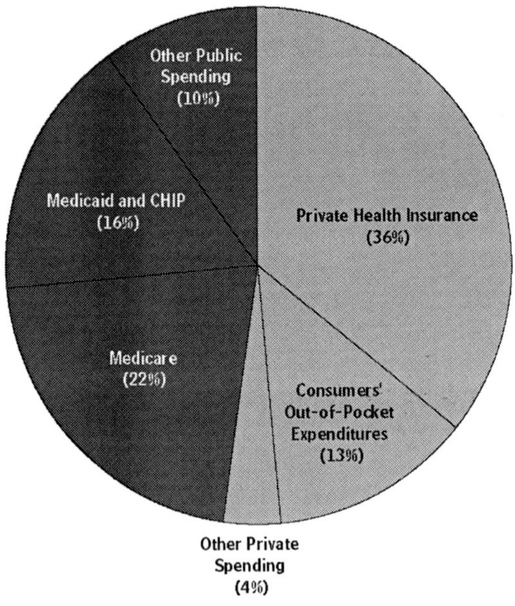

Source: Congressional Budget Office based on data from the Centers for Medicare and Medicaid Services.

Note: CHIP = Children's Health Insurance Program.

Figure 2.1. Distribution of Spending for Health Services and Supplies, 2008.

Even assuming that such changes occur, the Congressional Budget Office anticipates that federal spending on the government's major mandatory health care programs will continue to rise relative to GDP. CBO has projected spending for those programs—Medicare, Medicaid, the Children's Health Insurance Program, and the insurance subsidies that will be provided through exchanges established by the recently enacted health care legislation, described below—under two scenarios.[27] Under the extended-baseline scenario, which reflects current law, federal spending for those programs would grow from 5.5 percent of GDP today to about 10 percent of GDP in 2035; about 6 percent of GDP would be devoted to Medicare, and about 4 percent would be spent on Medicaid, CHIP, and the exchange subsidies. For the alternative fiscal scenario, CBO assumes that several policies designed to restrain federal spending on health care would not be continued. As a result, mandatory federal spending on health care programs would grow faster, reaching about 11 percent of GDP by 2035. Medicare spending would grow to about 7 percent of GDP, and federal spending on Medicaid, CHIP, and the exchange subsidies would reach about 4 percent of GDP. Beyond 2035, federal health care spending would continue to climb relative to GDP under both scenarios.

Quantifying the extent to which the rate of growth of health care spending will decline under current law is difficult. The growth of such spending relative to the growth of the economy has varied greatly from year to year during the past several decades, so projections of the likely difference in growth rates during the next few decades are very uncertain. As the projection period lengthens, the uncertainties mount because the likelihood of significant changes in medical practice and technology increases. As a result, CBO's projections of health care spending for the next few decades probably provide more real information than its projections for the longer term.

A new consideration in this year's *Long-Term Budget Outlook* is the recent enactment of the Patient Protection and Affordable Care Act, or PPACA (Public Law 111-148), and the Health Care and Education Reconciliation Act of 2010 (P.L. 111-152). That legislation has significant and conflicting implications for federal spending. On the one hand, it will substantially expand eligibility for Medicaid (mostly at federal expense) and provide subsidies through the new insurance exchanges. On the other hand, the legislation will significantly decrease Medicare outlays, largely by reducing payment rates for many types of health care providers relative to the rates that would have been paid under prior law, but also by making other specific changes in the program and establishing a mechanism designed to control the growth in Medicare's costs per enrollee. (The legislation made numerous other changes as well, but their impact on federal spending for health care is generally more modest.) The legislation will also increase federal revenues significantly (as discussed in Chapter 4); one noteworthy provision is a tax that will be imposed, starting in 2018, on employment-based health insurance plans with relatively high premiums, which will encourage enrollees in those plans to shift to less expensive and less extensive coverage.

CBO and the staff of the Joint Committee on Taxation (JCT) have estimated the budgetary effects of that legislation in detail for the next 10 years and in a much less precise way for the following 10 years.[28] The projections reported here incorporate that original estimate (except as modified to reflect different policies under the alternative fiscal scenario). Looking beyond the next two decades, determining the impact of the legislation on federal health care spending is very difficult because the uncertainties involved are so great. Moreover, disentangling the effects of the legislation from steps that would have been taken under prior law to slow the growth of health care spending becomes increasingly challenging. Consequently, CBO's approach in formulating the longer-term projections in this chapter has been to incorporate the projected effects of the legislation on the *level* of federal spending for health care over the next one or two decades (depending on the scenario) and to extrapolate such spending (including the incremental effects of the legislation) using the same *growth rates* that would have been applied in the absence of the legislation. The use of that mechanical approach reflects CBO's judgment that the agency does not have an analytic basis for projecting the effects of the recently enacted legislation on the growth rate of federal health care spending over the very long term.[29]

The projections presented in this chapter differ from those in last year's *Long-Term Budget Outlook* because of both technical changes in CBO's methodology and the impact of the health care legislation. In last year's report, CBO projected that mandatory federal spending on health care would total between 10 percent and 11 percent of GDP in 2035 under the extended-baseline scenario, slightly higher than the agency's current projection.[30] Under the alternative fiscal scenario, last year's projection for mandatory spending on health care was about 11 percent of GDP in 2035—essentially the same as the current projection.

Overview of Current Financing for Health Care

Although the recent health care legislation made a number of significant changes to Medicare, Medicaid, and the financing of private health insurance—and is projected to substantially reduce the number of people who are uninsured—reviewing the current status of the health insurance system is useful because it provides a starting point for CBO's projections.

Today, a combination of private and public sources finances the provision of health care in the United States. About 46 million people are covered by Medicare, and 58 million are covered by Medicaid, the two main sources of public financing.[31] Medicare provides near-universal coverage for the elderly and also covers several million nonelderly people; Medicaid covers a variety of low- income individuals, most of whom are nonelderly. The majority of Americans under the age of 65, however, have private health insurance. CBO estimates that about 150 million nonelderly people currently have an employment-based health plan as their primary source of coverage, and about 13 million people have primary insurance coverage purchased directly from an insurer. At any given time during this year, in CBO's estimation, about 50 million people will be uninsured.

In 2008, the most recent calendar year for which data are available, total spending for health care services and supplies amounted to about $2.2 trillion, or 15.1 percent of the nation's GDP.[32] In that year, 52 percent of spending was financed privately; the rest of the spending came from public sources (see Figure 2-1):

- Payments by private health insurers were the largest component of private spending, making up 36 percent of total expenditures on health care. Consumers' out- of-pocket expenses, which include payments made to satisfy deductibles and copayments for services covered by insurance, as well as payments for services not covered by insurance, accounted for 13 percent of those expenditures.[33] Other sources of private funds, such as philanthropy, accounted for 4 percent of total health care spending.
- Federal spending for Medicare made up 22 percent of total expenditures on health care in 2008, and federal and state spending for Medicaid and CHIP accounted for 16 percent. Another 10 percent was accounted for by various other public programs, including those run by state and local governments' health departments, the

Department of Veterans Affairs, the Department of Defense, and workers' compensation programs.

Medicare

In 2010, Medicare will provide federal health insurance for 46 million people who are elderly or disabled (the elderly make up nearly 85 percent of enrollees) or who have end-stage renal disease or amyotrophic lateral sclerosis (also known as Lou Gehrig's disease). People become eligible for Medicare on the basis of age when they reach 65; disabled individuals become eligible for the program 24 months after they qualify for benefits under Social Security's Disability Insurance program.

Part A of Medicare, or Hospital Insurance, primarily covers inpatient services provided by hospitals as well as skilled nursing and hospice care. Part B, or Supplementary Medical Insurance, mainly covers services provided by physicians and other practitioners and by hospitals' outpatient departments. Most enrollees in Medicare are in the traditional fee-for-service program, in which the federal government pays for covered services directly, but enrollees can instead obtain coverage for Medicare's benefits through a private health insurance plan under Part C of Medicare (called Medicare Advantage). A voluntary prescription drug benefit became available in 2006 as Part D of Medicare. In 2009, gross spending for Medicare was $499 billion.

The various parts of the program are financed in different ways. Part A benefits are financed primarily by a payroll tax (currently 2.9 percent of taxable earnings), the revenues from which are credited to the Hospital Insurance (HI) Trust Fund. For Part B, premiums paid by beneficiaries cover about one-quarter of outlays, and the government's general funds cover the rest. (Payments to private insurance plans under Part C are financed by a blend of funds from Parts A and B.) Enrollees' premiums under Part D are set to cover about one-quarter of the cost of the basic prescription drug benefit, although many low- income enrollees receive larger subsidies; general funds cover most of the remaining cost. Taking all of the parts of Medicare together, in calendar year 2008, about 42 percent of gross federal spending was financed by the payroll tax, about 12 percent by beneficiaries' premiums, and about 40 percent by general funds of the government.[34]

Cost-sharing requirements in Medicare vary widely, and the program does not set an annual cap on the amount of health care costs for which beneficiaries are responsible. However, the vast majority of beneficiaries who receive care in the fee-for-service portion of Medicare have supplemental insurance that covers many or all of the program's cost-sharing requirements.

According to one recent study, the most common sources of supplemental coverage in 2006 were plans for retirees offered by former employers (held by 39 percent of beneficiaries in the fee-for-service part of Medicare), individually purchased medigap policies (32 percent of beneficiaries), and Medicaid (16 percent) .[9]

Medicaid and CHIP

Medicaid is a joint federal/state program that pays for health care services for a variety of low-income individuals. In 2009, federal spending for Medicaid was $251 billion, of which $228 billion covered benefits for enrollees. (In addition to benefits, Medicaid's spending included payments to hospitals that treat a "disproportionate share" of low-income patients, costs for the Vaccines for Children program, and administrative expenses.) The federal government's share of Medicaid's spending for benefits varies among the states. That share usually averages 57 percent, but legislation temporarily boosted it in response to the economic downturn; in 2009, the federal share averaged two-thirds. According to the Centers for Medicare and Medicaid Services, states spent $130 billion on Medicaid in 2009.

States administer their Medicaid programs under federal guidelines that specify a minimum set of services that must be provided to certain categories of low-income individuals. Required services include inpatient and outpatient hospital services, services provided by physicians and laboratories, and nursing home and home health care. To be eligible for Medicaid, a person must have a low income and (in certain cases) only a few assets— although the minimum financial thresholds vary, depending on the basis for an enrollee's eligibility. Groups that must be eligible include low-income children and families who would have qualified for the former Aid to Families with Dependent Children program, certain other low- income children and pregnant women, and most elderly and disabled individuals who qualify for the Supplemental Security Income program.

Within those requirements and other statutory limits, states have flexibility in administering the Medicaid program and determining its scope. Partly as a result, the program's rules are complex, and it is difficult to generalize about the types of enrollees covered, the benefits offered, and the cost sharing required. States may choose to make additional groups of people eligible (such as individuals with income above the mandatory eligibility thresholds and those who have high medical expenses relative to their income) or to provide additional benefits (such as coverage for prescription drugs and dental services), and they have exercised those options to varying degrees. Moreover, many states seek and receive federal waivers that allow them to provide benefits and cover groups that would otherwise be excluded. By one estimate, federal and state expenditures on optional populations and benefits accounted for about 60 percent of the Medicaid program's total spending in 2001.[35]

About 71 million people will be enrolled in Medicaid at some point during 2010, CBO estimates; the average enrollment over the course of the year will be about 58 million. Those two ways of measuring enrollment yield such divergent estimates because many people are eligible for Medicaid for only part of the year. About half of Medicaid's enrollees are low-income children, and another one-quarter are either the parents of those children or low-income pregnant women. The elderly and disabled constitute the remaining one-quarter of Medicaid's enrollees. Expenses tend to be higher for elderly and disabled beneficiaries, many of whom require long-term care, than for other beneficiaries. About one-third of Medicaid's spending is for long-term care, which includes nursing home services, home health care, and other medical and social services for people whose disabilities prevent them from living independently. Overall, the elderly and disabled account for about two-thirds of the program's spending.

CHIP is a joint federal/state program that provides health insurance coverage for uninsured children living in families with income that is relatively low but too high for them to qualify for Medicaid.[36] Like Medicaid, CHIP is administered by the states within broad federal guidelines. Unlike Medicaid, however, CHIP is a matching Henry J. Kaiser Family Foundation, June 2005), p. 11. grant program with a fixed nationwide cap on federal spending. In 2009, federal spending on CHIP was $7.5 billion, and about 8 million people (mostly children) were enrolled in the program at some point during the year. The federal share of CHIP spending varies among the states but usually averages 70 percent.

The Historical Growth of Health Care Spending

Total spending for health care in the United States—that is, private and public spending combined—has risen significantly as a share of GDP over the past several decades. Such spending has grown relative to GDP in most years, with the notable exception of the period from 1993 to 2000, when spending for health care remained relatively stable as a share of the economy. Many analysts have attributed that lull in growth to a substantial rise in the number of people enrolled in managed care plans as well as to excess capacity among some types of providers, which increased the leverage that health plans had in negotiating payments. Economic growth was also relatively rapid in that period.

Spending for Medicare and Medicaid has also grown quickly in recent decades, in part because of rising enrollment and in part because of rising costs per enrollee. Between 1975 and 2009, gross federal spending for Medicare rose from 0.9 percent of GDP to 3.5 percent, and federal spending for Medicaid increased from 0.4 percent of GDP to 1.8 percent. Over that same period, total spending for Medicaid (including spending by the states) increased from 0.8 percent of GDP to 2.7 percent.

Underlying Factors

A crucial factor underlying the rise in per capita spending for health care in recent decades has been the emergence, adoption, and widespread diffusion of new medical technologies and services.[37] Major advances in medical science allow providers to diagnose and treat illnesses in ways that previously were impossible. Many of those innovations rely on costly new drugs, equipment, and skills. Other innovations are relatively inexpensive, but their costs add up quickly as growing numbers of providers and patients make use of them. Although technological advances can sometimes reduce costs, in medicine such advances and the resulting changes in clinical practice have generally increased spending.

Other factors that have contributed to the growth of per capita health care spending include increases in personal income and the expanded scope of health insurance coverage. Demand for medical care tends to rise as real (inflation-adjusted) family income increases. Moreover, the expanding scope of insurance coverage in recent decades, as evidenced by the substantial reduction in the percentage of health care costs that people pay out of pocket, has also increased demand, because insurance coverage reduces the cost of medical care for consumers. (The share of the population with health insurance has declined slightly in recent decades.) Spending on health care would also be expected to grow if people were developing more health problems or were becoming more likely to contract diseases, but the evidence on whether those factors have substantially increased the use of health care in the past few decades is mixed.[38]

Disentangling the effects of technology, income, and insurance on the growth of health care spending is difficult because the growth of income and insurance coverage has increased the demand for new technologies. A recent study estimated that new medical technologies and rising income were the most important factors explaining the growth in health care spending since 1960, with the two accounting for similar shares of that growth.[39] But the study also noted that the effect of the expansion in insurance coverage on spending growth is highly uncertain. Another recent study concluded that the expansion of insurance coverage resulting from the introduction of Medicare had a substantial impact on national health care spending—raising costs not just for the elderly patients who gained coverage but for nonelderly patients as well. It attributed part of the impact to more rapid and widespread adoption of existing treatment methods (such as those provided by cardiac intensive care units), but questions remain about the magnitude of those effects.[40]

Studies that have analyzed the sources of past spending growth have consistently found that the aging of the population has had only a small effect. Although older adults generally have higher average medical expenses than younger adults, the age composition of the population has not changed sufficiently to account for much of the increase in per capita spending. Aging has had a larger effect on federal spending for health care, however, because nearly all U.S. residents become eligible for Medicare when they turn 65. Over the past four decades, the share of the population that was age 65 or older grew by about one-quarter—from 10 percent to 13 percent.

Excess Cost Growth

When analyzing historical trends in the growth of health care spending and developing projections for future growth of that spending, it is useful to distinguish between various components of that growth. As part of that analysis, it is common to calculate the increase in health care spending per person relative to the growth of GDP per person after removing the effects of demographic changes on health care spending—in particular, changes in the population's age distribution. The remaining difference in growth rates is generally referred to as "excess cost growth." The phrase is not intended to imply that growth in per capita spending for health care is necessarily excessive or undesirable; it simply measures the extent to which the growth in such spending (adjusting for changes in the age composition of the population) exceeds the growth in per capita GDP.[41]

The resulting calculations indicate that rates of excess cost growth have ranged between 1.0 and 2.5 percentage points across programs and during various time periods between 1975 and 2008 (see Table 2-1). For all categories of health care spending, excess cost growth was greater, on average, during the 1975–2008 period than during the 1990–2008 period. Average annual rates of excess cost growth for total health care spending during those two periods were 1.9 percentage points and 1.4 percentage points, respectively.

CBO's Projection Methodology

This section reviews the approach that CBO follows in projecting mandatory federal spending on health care over the long term and discusses some technical changes in the application of that approach that have been made since last year's report. The ways in which the effects of the recently enacted health care legislation have been incorporated into the projections are examined in a subsequent section, after the key provisions of that legislation have been described more fully. In effect, the current section describes how CBO would have projected spending for health care in the absence of that legislation—which serves as the starting point for incorporating the impact of the legislation.

For the first 10 years of the projection period, CBO uses the estimates of spending for Medicare and Medicaid from its most recent baseline budget projections, which reflect a detailed analysis of each program and its components. (Throughout this analysis, spending on CHIP, which accounts for less than 0.1 percent of GDP, is combined with spending on Medicaid.) For the years beyond that 10-year span, CBO uses the projected amounts of spending in the last year of the baseline (2020) and applies growth rates that reflect CBO's projections of income growth, general inflation, and demographic changes, as well as rates of excess cost growth that initially reflect historical growth rates but that are assumed to slow over time. [42] Thus, two of the key parameters that affect the projections of mandatory federal spending on health care are the initial rates of excess cost growth and the path by which those rates diminish.

Initial Rates of Excess Cost Growth

Given the uncertainty surrounding future trends in cost growth for health care, a reasonable starting point is the historical rate of excess cost growth. Use of that starting point is consistent with the assumption that the future will look like the past, at least initially. Selecting which historical period to use, however, presents a trade-off: Using a longer period avoids giving transient or cyclical developments undue weight, but it also gives too little emphasis to more-recent trends that turn out to be persistent.

Table 2.1. Excess Cost Growth in Spending for Health Care.

(Percentage points)				
	Medicare	**Medicaid**	**All Other**	**Total**
1975 to 2008	2.5	2.0	1.8	1.9
1980 to 2008	2.2	1.7	1.9	1.9
1985 to 2008	1.5	1.2	1.8	1.7
1990 to 2008	1.8	1.0	1.4	1.4

Source: Congressional Budget Office.

Note: Excess cost growth refers to the extent to which the growth rate of Medicare or Medicaid spending per beneficiary—or all other health care spending per capita—exceeded the growth rate of nominal gross domestic product per capita per year, on average.

The long-term projections in this chapter are based on the average rate of excess cost growth observed between 1985 and 2008. Excess cost growth was lower, on average, during that period than during the longer 1975–2008 period. That slowing probably stems, at least in part, from two important shifts: Private health insurance moved away from indemnity policies—which generally reimburse enrollees for their incurred medical costs, and which predominated before the 1990s—and toward greater management of care; and Medicare shifted from cost-based payment methods to fee schedules that seem less conducive to spending growth because price increases are constrained. Excess cost growth was even lower, on average, during the shorter 1990–2008 period, but that average gives a good deal of weight to the years in the 1 990s when managed care was spreading most rapidly— some of which probably represented a one-time downward shift in health care costs rather than a change in the underlying growth rate. In CBO's judgment, the average rate of excess cost growth since 1985 best reflects features of the health care and health insurance systems that are likely to endure.

CBO used the average rate of excess cost growth since 1985 for total health care spending—1.7 percentage points—as the initial rate for Medicare, Medicaid, and all other national health care spending, rather than starting from those sectors' differing historical rates. That approach recognizes that past changes in federal law have affected the growth rates observed in Medicare and Medicaid to an extent that is difficult to disentangle from other factors affecting those growth rates. It also reflects the considerable uncertainty about whether and how future growth rates will differ across the sectors.

This approach to developing initial growth rates differs from that adopted in CBO's June 2009 *Long-Term Budget Outlook* in two ways: The projections for last year's report were based on trends since 1975, and they used the differing historical growth rates for each of the three sectors as those sectors' starting points.

Path of the Slowdown

When health care expenditures increase as a share of GDP, they absorb a rising share of people's income, reducing growth in the consumption of other goods and services. Thus, continued growth in health care spending will create mounting pressure to slow the growth of costs, even in the absence of changes in federal law.

The private sector and state governments will probably respond to rising costs for health care by instituting various changes. Employers can intensify their efforts to reduce the costs of the insurance plans they sponsor—for example, by working with insurers to make the delivery of health care more efficient or by reducing the extent of the insurance coverage they offer. To avoid higher premiums, employees can shift to plans with more tightly managed benefits or higher cost-sharing requirements. State governments can respond to growing costs for Medicaid by limiting the services they choose to cover or by tightening eligibility to reduce the number of beneficiaries. Because the federal government's spending for Medicaid depends on what the states spend, actions by the states that reduce the growth of their Medicaid spending will also slow the growth of federal spending for the program.

Many features of the Medicare program cannot be altered without changes in federal law. Still, a slowdown in spending growth outside of Medicare will affect Medicare, which is integrated to a significant degree with the rest of the health care system. In particular, Medicare will probably experience some reduction in cost growth to the extent that actions by individuals, businesses, and states result in lower-cost "patterns of practice" by physicians, slower development and diffusion of new technologies, and cost-limiting changes to the structure of the overall health care system. Moreover, the federal government will probably make regulatory changes aimed at slowing the growth of spending for Medicare (and Medicaid), and the demand for health care services by Medicare beneficiaries will be constrained as the program's premiums and cost- sharing amounts consume a growing share of beneficiaries' income.

In the absence of changes in federal law, state governments and the private sector have more flexibility to respond to the pressures of rising health care spending than does the federal government. Consequently, CBO projects that excess cost growth in Medicaid's spending and in other (non-Medicaid, non-Medicare) spending would slow to a greater degree than would Medicare's spending. Specifically, CBO assumed that the rate of excess cost growth for both Medicaid and other health care spending in 2084 (the last year of the current 75-year projection period) would be zero, whereas the rate of excess cost growth for Medicare at the end of the period would be 1.0 percentage point. Excess cost growth is projected to decline linearly—that is, by the same fractional number of percentage points each year—from its initial starting point of 1.7 percentage points. That approach reflects a judgment that, over time, the steps needed to keep reducing growth rates will become increasingly onerous but that the pressure to take them will also intensify because of continued increases in health care spending.

That approach to specifying the path of the slowdown in excess cost growth differs from the approach adopted in last year's report in two ways: The projected values of excess cost growth in the final year of the projection period differ slightly, and last year's report projected that the reductions in growth rates would occur relatively quickly in the initial years and more slowly in the later years.[43]

Resulting Growth Rates

Under CBO's approach, excess cost growth projected for the 2021-2084 period averages about 0.8 percentage points for Medicaid and for other health care spending and about 1.3 percentage points for Medicare. That is, in the absence of changes in federal law, Medicare's costs per enrollee are projected to grow—on average over a 65-year period—about 0.5 percentage points faster than either per-enrollee costs in the Medicaid program or per capita costs for other spending on health care. (Those calculations do not factor in any effects of the recent health care legislation, which are examined below.) In last year's projections, that gap was larger. Specifically, the average rates projected for excess cost growth over a similar period were 0.6 percentage points for Medicaid, 0.5 percentage points for other spending, and 1.5 percentage points for Medicare.

It might be difficult to envision how excess cost growth in Medicare's spending could continually outstrip spending for Medicaid and other health care over such a long period. One way in which that might happen is that actions taken to reduce spending growth in the private sector could weaken the incentives to develop and diffuse new medical technologies for nonelderly people but have less of an effect on new technologies focused on diseases that principally affect the elderly. Indeed, excess cost growth in Medicare has exceeded that for other spending by as much as half a percentage point over periods of a few decades, even though past growth rates reflect changes in law that have probably helped to slow growth in Medicare's costs; noticeable differences in future growth rates over such periods would not be unprecedented.

Relative to a projection in which excess cost growth persists at historical rates, the sizable slowdown in excess cost growth that CBO projects probably can be achieved only through significant changes in the nature of health care, access to care, or the amount that households pay directly for care. For example, in the private sector, households will probably face increased cost sharing; new and potentially useful health technologies will probably be introduced more slowly or be used less frequently than they would without a slowdown in excess cost growth; and more treatments and interventions may simply not be covered by insurance. In addition, households that would otherwise receive health insurance through Medicaid may be ineligible because of tightened eligibility rules or may be eligible but find that the scope of covered services has been reduced. Even so, health care costs are projected to continue to rise more rapidly than income, representing an increasing share of total output and of federal spending.

Summary of Initial Assessments

Without taking into account the impact of the recently enacted health care legislation, CBO's long-term projections of health care spending would be based on the following set of assessments:

- Spending for Medicare and Medicaid from 2010 through 2020 would equal the projections in CBO's most recent baseline (which did not include the effects of the recent legislation).
- In 2021, excess cost growth in spending for Medicare, Medicaid, and all other health care spending would equal the overall average for historical growth since 1985—that is, 1.7 percentage points.
- Excess cost growth in all three categories—Medicare, Medicaid, and other health care spending—would slow beginning in 2022.
- Excess cost growth for Medicare would decline linearly from 1.7 percentage points in 2021 to 1.0 percentage point in 2084, and excess cost growth for Medicaid and for health care spending apart from Medicare and Medicaid would decline linearly from 1.7 percentage points in 2021 to zero in 2084.

Recent Health Care Legislation

Lawmakers enacted legislation in March 2010 that will substantially change the nation's health insurance system and have significant implications for federal spending on health care. The Patient Protection and Affordable Care Act, as amended by the Health Care and Education Reconciliation Act of 2010, will require most legal residents of the United States to obtain health insurance starting in 2014; significantly expand eligibility for Medicaid; set up insurance exchanges through which certain individuals and families will receive federal subsidies to greatly reduce their cost of purchasing private coverage; substantially reduce the growth of Medicare's payment rates for most services (relative to the growth rates projected under prior law); impose an excise tax on insurance plans with relatively high premiums; and make various other changes to the federal tax code, Medicare, Medicaid, and other programs.

Provisions That Will Increase Federal Spending

The expansion of Medicaid eligibility and the provision of subsidies through the new insurance exchanges will both increase federal spending for health care. Starting in 2014, most nonelderly people with income below 138 percent of the federal poverty level (FPL) will become eligible for Medicaid.[44] The people who will gain eligibility for Medicaid under the new law consist primarily of nonelderly adults with low income who are not parents of dependent children. (Low-income children and their parents already qualify for Medicaid under prior law, although the income thresholds vary by state.) The federal government will pay all of the costs of covering newly eligible enrollees through 2016. In subsequent years, the federal share of that spending will decline gradually to 90 percent in 2020, where it will remain.

Insurance exchanges will be established in 2014 through which certain people with income up to 400 percent of the FPL will be eligible for federal subsidies to reduce their cost of obtaining private health insurance coverage. Eligible people who purchase a relatively inexpensive plan providing a specified level of benefits will receive a subsidy that limits their net premium to a certain percentage of their income. In 2014, the percentages of income will range from 2 percent for the lowest-income households to 9.5 percent for households with income between 300 percent and 400 percent of the FPL (those percentages will be indexed in future years, as described below). People with income below 250 percent of the FPL will also be eligible to receive subsidies to reduce their cost- sharing requirements. People will not be eligible to receive subsidies through the exchanges if they already qualify for public coverage—including Medicaid—or if they are offered coverage through their employment, unless they would have to pay more than a specified share of their income for such coverage.

Although the premium subsidies are structured as tax credits, most of the funds involved will be classified as outlays because their value will often exceed what enrollees' income tax liability would otherwise be.[45] In addition, the subsidies to reduce enrollees' cost sharing will be classified as outlays.

Provisions That Will Reduce Federal Spending

The legislation contains a number of provisions that will substantially reduce federal spending on Medicare relative to what it would have been under prior law. The major source of those savings is a set of provisions that permanently reduce the annual updates to Medicare's payment rates for many types of fee-for-service health care providers. Under prior law, those payment updates would have generally been equal to the estimated change in the average cost of providers' inputs (such as labor and equipment). Under the new law, however, those updates will be adjusted downward by the estimated rate of economy- wide growth in productivity—a measure that seeks to capture, for the economy as a whole, how much more output is being produced from a given level of inputs. (In some cases, the law also specifies additional reductions in the update factors.) The other key source of savings, according to CBO's projections, is a reduction in payments to private health insurance plans under Part C of Medicare.

The legislation also includes various changes in Medicare's payment policies that many experts believe have the potential to reduce federal spending on health care without harming patients' health—but that CBO expects will probably require much experimentation and refinement before significant savings will be achieved. Therefore, CBO projected limited savings during the next two decades from provisions allowing physicians to establish "accountable care organizations," establishing a national pilot program to develop approaches to bundling the payments for an "episode" of care during and after hospitalization, and making related changes to other payment policies.[46] The legislation further establishes a Center for Medicare and Medicaid Innovation and gives the Secretary of Health and Human Services broad authority to develop and conduct experiments to test and refine new approaches to paying providers and delivering health care benefits. The Secretary has the authority to implement such approaches on a broader scale (including nationally) if an evaluation concludes that they have favorable effects on the quality of care and expenditures.

In addition, the legislation establishes an Independent Payment Advisory Board (IPAB), which will be required to submit proposals to reduce Medicare's spending per enrollee if the growth of such spending is projected to exceed certain targets. Those proposals would go into effect automatically unless blocked or replaced by subsequent legislative action. From 2015 through 2019, the target growth rate is the average of general price inflation and measured price inflation for medical services. In subsequent years, the target growth rate is the percentage increase in per capita GDP plus 1 percentage point. The legislation places a number of limitations on the actions available to the IPAB, including a prohibition against modifying Medicare's eligibility rules or reducing benefits. Nevertheless, CBO expects these provisions to restrain Medicare spending somewhat.

The legislation also imposes an excise tax on relatively expensive insurance plans offered through employers, starting in 2018. The primary impact of that tax on the federal budget is through federal revenues, as discussed in Chapter 4; whether and how it will affect federal spending for health care (for example, through spillovers from changes in private spending for health care) is difficult to predict.

Questions About Sustainabiity

One challenge that arises in projecting federal outlays for health care over the long term is that the recent legislation either left in place or put into effect a number of procedures that may be difficult to sustain over a long period. For example, the legislation did not alter the sustainable growth rate mechanism used for determining updates to Medicare's payment rates for physicians; under that mechanism, those rates are scheduled to be reduced by about 21 percent in 2010 and then decline further in subsequent years. Since that mechanism was enacted in 1997, its provisions have usually been modified to avoid scheduled reductions in payment rates, and legislation was just enacted to delay cuts in those payment rates until December 2010 (a development that is not reflected in the projections). At the same time, the legislation includes provisions that will constrain payment rates for other providers of Medicare's services. In particular, increases in payment rates for many providers will be held below the rate of increase in the average cost of providers' inputs.

Taking all the provisions of the legislation together, CBO expects that, adjusted for inflation, Medicare spending per beneficiary will increase at an average annual rate of less than 2 percent during the next two decades—

compared with a roughly 4 percent annual growth rate during the past two decades (a calculation that excludes the effect of establishing the Medicare prescription drug benefit). It is unclear whether that lower rate of growth can be sustained and, if so, whether it will be accomplished through greater efficiencies in the delivery of health care or will instead reduce access to care or diminish the quality of care (relative to the situation under prior law).

Another provision that may be difficult to sustain will slow the growth of federal subsidies for health insurance purchased through the insurance exchanges. For enrollees who receive subsidies, the amount they will have to pay depends primarily on a formula that determines what share of their income they have to contribute to enroll in a relatively low-cost plan (with the subsidy covering the difference between that contribution and the total premium for that plan). Initially, the percentages of income that enrollees must pay are indexed so that the subsidies will cover roughly the same share of the total premium over time. After 2018, however, an additional indexing factor will probably apply; if so, the shares of income that enrollees have to pay will increase more rapidly, and the shares of the premium that the subsidies cover will decline.[47]

Net Budgetary Effects of the Legislation

CBO and the staff of the Joint Committee on Taxation have provided detailed estimates of the effects of the recently enacted health care legislation on the federal budget over the period from 2010 to 2019 and have provided a less precise analysis for the subsequent decade.[48] Those estimates show an increase in mandatory outlays of $382 billion and an increase in federal revenues of $525 billion over the 2010–2019 period, yielding a reduction in deficits of $143 billion. CBO and JCT expect that the legislation will also reduce federal budget deficits over the ensuing decade relative to those projected under prior law—with a total effect during that decade in a broad range around 0.5 percent of GDP. The imprecision of that calculation reflects the even greater degree of uncertainty that attends to it, compared with the 10-year budget estimates. Federal outlays for health care are projected to remain higher than they would have been under prior law for most of that second decade, but to fall slightly below the prior-law level by 2030 (under the assumption that all of the legislation's provisions are fully implemented).[49]

Determining the effects of the legislation beyond 2030 is very difficult because of the considerable uncertainties involved. A wide range of changes could occur—in people's health, in the sources and extent of their insurance coverage, and in the delivery of medical care—that are almost impossible to predict but that could have a significant effect on federal health care spending, both under the legislation and under prior law. Furthermore, over a longer time horizon, it becomes very challenging to disentangle the effects of the legislation from the effects of other changes that would have been made even without the legislation to slow the growth of private and public spending on health care.

Because the legislation is expected to reduce mandatory federal spending on health care 20 years from now, the average growth rate of that spending calculated over those two decades will be slightly lower than it would otherwise have been. It might seem natural to assume that the difference in growth rates will continue indefinitely, but that sort of extrapolation may not be appropriate. Distinguishing between a series of shifts in the level of federal health care spending and permanent changes in the growth rate of such spending is difficult. Although CBO can provide a rough indication of the legislation's effect on the level of spending 20 years ahead, the agency does not believe that it has an analytic basis for evaluating whether the legislation's effect on the rate of growth of spending over the next 20 years will continue.

Therefore, to project mandatory federal spending on health care for the longer term—incorporating the impact of the new laws—CBO has adopted a relatively simple and mechanical approach. Specifically, the projections incorporate the effects of the legislation on the *level* of that spending over the next one or two decades and then calculate spending in subsequent years by applying the same *growth rates* that would have applied in the absence of the legislation. In other words, the incremental effects of the legislation are extrapolated using the same growth rates as are projected in the absence of the legislation. Consequently, because the legislation is expected to reduce Medicare's spending by about 20 percent in 2030, projected Medicare spending will be about 20 percent lower than the prior-law projections in subsequent years. Likewise, because the legislation is estimated to raise Medicaid's spending by about 20 percent in 2030, Medicaid's spending is projected to remain about 20 percent above the prior-law estimates thereafter.

Long-Term Projections of Mandatory Federal Spending

CBO calculated mandatory federal spending on health care under two scenarios. The first is intended to reflect the provisions of current law; the second deviates from current law:

- Under the extended-baseline scenario, the effects of the recent health care legislation as estimated by CBO and JCT for the next two decades are layered on top of CBO's March 2010 baseline projections. Medicare's payment rates for physicians are assumed to be reduced as specified under current law through 2020. Beyond the next 20 years, the projected growth rates in spending for the government's mandatory health care programs are based on CBO's projections of demographic and economic trends (see Appendix B) and the agency's projections about excess cost growth for the 2030–2084 period.
- Under the alternative fiscal scenario, the effects of the recent health care legislation as estimated by CBO and JCT for the next decade are layered on top of CB O's March 2010 baseline projections—except that Medicare's payment rates for physicians are assumed to rise gradually through 2020.[50] Beyond that point, the projected growth rates in spending for the government's mandatory health care programs are based on CBO's projections of demographic and economic trends and the agency's projections about excess cost growth for the 2021–2084 period.

The two scenarios thus differ in only one respect through 2020: Under the extended-baseline scenario, the existing sustainable growth rate formula used to determine payment rates for physicians is assumed to continue to apply, resulting in sharp reductions in those payment rates from the current amounts; under the alternative fiscal scenario, Medicare's payment rates for physicians are instead assumed to increase gradually, pushing up total spending. The resulting difference between the scenarios regarding physicians' payments by Medicare during the first 10 years affects the projections of Medicare's spending beyond 2020 as well.

Between 2020 and 2030, the difference between the two scenarios is greater. Under the extended-baseline scenario, projected federal spending is assumed to be constrained by a number of policies specified in the recent health care legislation—the continuing reductions in updates for Medicare's payment rates, the constraints on Medicare imposed by the IPAB, and the additional indexing provision that will slow the growth of exchange subsidies after 2018. Because those policies may be difficult to maintain over the long term, in the alternative fiscal scenario it is assumed that they will not continue after 2020. Given CBO's projection methodology, the upshot of those assumptions is that federal spending would be higher in 2030 under the alternative fiscal scenario and would grow at the same rate under both scenarios thereafter.[51] The resulting difference between the extended-baseline scenario and the alternative fiscal scenario highlights the significance of those policies for the federal budget.

The subsidies provided through the new insurance exchanges are projected differently under the two scenarios. For the extended-baseline scenario, those outlays are extrapolated through 2029 in a way that is consistent with the cost estimate for the health care legislation. For the alternative fiscal scenario, outlays are projected through 2029 in a similar manner but without applying the additional indexing provision that would reduce the government's share of premium costs (described on page 37). For each scenario, projections for outlays beyond 2029 are based on CBO's projections of demographic and economic trends and the agency's projections of excess cost growth for Medicaid and all other health care spending over the 2030–2084 period.

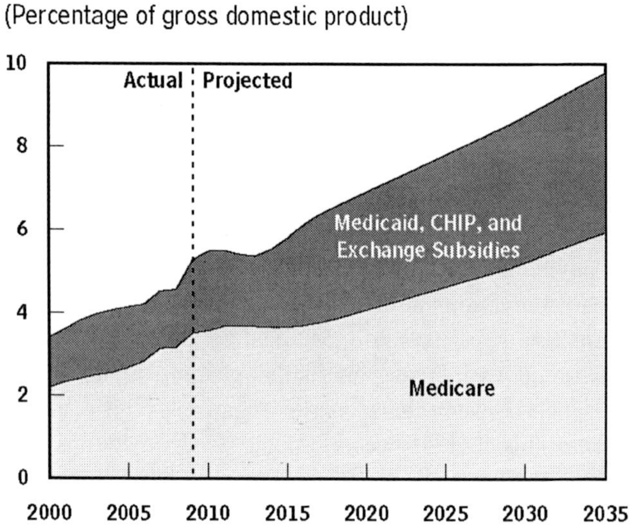

Source: Congressional Budget Office.

Notes: The extended-baseline scenario adheres closely to current law, following CBO's 10-year baseline budget projections through 2020 (with adjustments for the recently enacted health care legislation) and then extending the baseline concept for the rest of the long-term projection period. (For details, see Table 1-1 on page 3.)

CHIP = Children's Health Insurance Program.

Figure 2.2. Mandatory Federal Spending on Health Care, by Category, Under CBO's Extended-Baseline Scenario.

In both scenarios, the projections of exchange subsidies are subject to an especially large degree of uncertainty and could err in either direction. On the one hand, income growth and the indexing of the subsidies may diminish the value of the exchange subsidies over time; on the other hand, changes in other insurance options (including employment-based insurance) could cause spending on exchange subsidies to grow faster than projected. In all of the projections, the outlays for exchange subsidies are presented in combination with outlays for Medicaid (and CHIP) both for ease of exposition and to reflect the fact that they all constitute federal subsidies to provide health insurance for lower- and moderate-income households. (Most of the exchange subsidies are classified as outlays; the portion that reflects reductions in revenue is included in the revenue projections discussed in Chapter 4.)

Projected Spending

In 2010, federal spending on Medicare, Medicaid, and CHIP will amount to 5.5 percent of GDP, CBO expects, with Medicare accounting for 3.6 percent of GDP and federal spending on Medicaid and CHIP adding 1.9 percent of GDP.

Under the extended-baseline scenario, federal spending for those programs and for the exchange subsidies would total about 10 percent of GDP in 2035; about 6 percent would be for Medicare, and about 4 percent would be for Medicaid, CHIP, and the exchange subsidies (see Figure 2-2). Extrapolating to 2080, total federal spending on those major health care programs would reach about 17 percent of GDP: Medicare's share would be between 11 percent and 12 percent, and the share for Medicaid, CHIP, and the exchange subsidies would be between 5 percent and 6 percent.[52] The figures for 2080 should be viewed with much more caution because of the greater uncertainty involved in making such long-range projections.

Under the alternative fiscal scenario, mandatory federal spending on the major health care programs would be higher because CBO assumed that several policies designed to limit that spending would not continue in effect; as a result, projected spending would be greater, particularly for Medicare, than under the extended-baseline scenario. Specifically, Medicare's spending would grow to about 7 percent of GDP by 2035, and federal spending on Medicaid, CHIP, and the exchange subsidies would reach about 4 percent of GDP—so total federal spending on those programs would be about 11 percent of GDP (see Figure 2-3). Extrapolating to 2080, federal spending on those programs would continue to rise, reaching about 19 percent of GDP. Medicare's spending would be between 13 percent and 14 percent of GDP, or about 2 percentage points higher than under the extended-baseline scenario. Federal spending for Medicaid, CHIP, and the exchange subsidies in 2080 would be between 5 percent and 6 percent of GDP—close to the amount estimated under the extended-baseline scenario, because the policies governing Medicaid and CHIP are the same in both cases and because exchange subsidies represent a relatively small share of GDP. (For CBO's projections of national spending on health care, see Box 2-1 on page 42.)

Comparison with CBO's 2009 Projections

In last year's report, CBO projected that mandatory federal spending on the major health care programs would total between 10 percent and 11 percent of GDP in 2035 under the extended-baseline scenario, slightly higher than the agency's current projection.[53] That total was projected to rise to about 19 percent of GDP by 2080 in last year's report, about 2 percentage points higher than the current projection. Under the alternative fiscal scenario, last year's projection for mandatory federal spending on health care was about 11 percent of GDP in 2035 and was between 19 percent and 20 percent of GDP in 2080—roughly the same as the current projections.

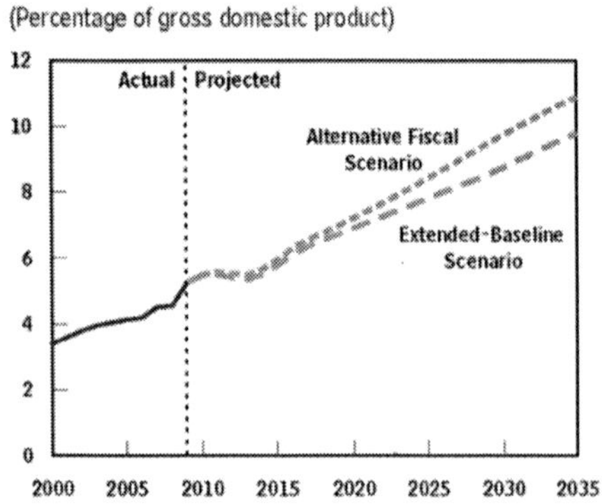

Source: Congressional Budget Office.

Note: The extended-baseline scenario adheres closely to current law, following CBO's 10-year baseline budget projections through 2020 (with adjustments for the recently enacted health care legislation) and then extending the baseline concept for the rest of the long-term projection period. The alternative fiscal scenario incorporates several changes to current law that are widely expected to occur or that would modify some provisions that might be difficult to sustain for a long period. (For details, see Table 1-1 on page 3.)

Figure 2.3. Mandatory Federal Spending on Health Care Under CBO's Long-Term Budget Scenarios.

The differences from last year's projections reflect both technical changes in CBO's methodology and the impact of the recently enacted health care legislation. For the extended-baseline scenario, CBO's technical changes reduced projected federal spending on health care through 2035, compared with last year's projection.

The net impact of the recent legislation was to increase federal spending for most of the next 20 years; but by 2035, the incremental effect of the legislation (if all of its provisions are fully implemented) is a net reduction in projected expenditures (see Figure 2-4 on page 44). By that point, the savings in Medicare are expected to exceed the combined increase in outlays for Medicaid, CHIP, and the exchange subsidies. Even so, most of the difference from last year's projection for 2035 is attributable to CBO's technical changes rather than the effects of the legislation. For the alternative fiscal scenario, the net effect of CBO's technical changes was about the same as for the extended-baseline scenario. However, under that scenario, the net impact of the recent legislation would be to increase federal spending in 2035 because of the assumption that a number of important provisions of the legislation that would reduce federal spending would not continue in effect beyond 2020.

Under both scenarios, the relatively small net changes in mandatory federal spending on health care relative to last year's projections mask larger gross differences in projected spending on Medicare, Medicaid, CHIP, and the exchange subsidies. Specifically, under the extended- baseline scenario, gross Medicare spending in 2035 is now projected to be lower by nearly 2 percent of GDP, compared with last year's projections, and outlays for Medicaid, CHIP, and the new exchange subsidies are higher by about 1 percent of GDP.[54] (Again, those differences in the component projections reflect both technical changes and the effects of legislation.) By 2080, the differences from last year's projections are larger—gross Medicare spending is lower in this year's projection, by about 4 percent of GDP, and spending for Medicaid, CHIP, and the exchange subsidies is higher, by about 2 percent of GDP. Those results largely reflect CB O's judgment that Medicare's spending will grow at a somewhat faster rate than Medicaid's after 2030; consequently, the savings from reducing projected Medicare spending in 2030 become magnified over time relative to the added costs projected for Medicaid, CHIP, and the exchange subsidies.

Projections Under Alternative Assumptions

Although all long-term economic and demographic trends are uncertain and thus difficult to forecast, excess cost growth in health care spending during the next 75 years may be particularly so. The systems of health care and health care financing have existed in their current forms for only a few decades, and medical technology continues to evolve rapidly. The projections in this chapter will undoubtedly prove to be inaccurate in one direction or another. And judging their accuracy will be difficult even after the fact, because they assume no changes in federal law or policies, and such changes are virtually certain to occur. Even without policy changes, though, actual spending for health care could be much lower or much higher than the figures contained in CBO's and other forecasters' projections.

For comparison purposes, CBO projected federal spending for Medicare, Medicaid, CHIP, and the exchange subsidies under varying assumptions about excess cost growth. The effects of that variation are easiest to illustrate by changing the rate of excess cost growth that applies after 2020 under the alternative fiscal scenario. A projection in which such growth is held constant at zero, although implausible, is useful because it isolates the effect that the aging of the population has on spending (see Figure 2-5 on page 45). In that case, mandatory federal spending on health care would increase from 5.5 percent of GDP in 2010 to nearly 9 percent by 2035.

Box 2-1. National Spending on Health Care

The Congressional Budget Office (CBO) has a limited ability to project national spending on health care because the agency does not track several components of those expenditures as closely as it analyzes the components that are part of the federal budget. To generate projections of total expenditures on health care over the longer term, the agency has combined its own projections with estimates and projections developed by the Office of the Actuary in the Centers for Medicare and Medicaid Services (CMS).[1] The projections are rough and involve substantial uncertainty—especially those that extend far into the future—and thus should be viewed with caution.

During the past 30 years, total spending on health care has almost doubled as a share of the economy, growing from 8 percent to 15 percent of gross domestic product (GDP). To project such spending in the future, CBO developed two scenarios.

Under the extended-baseline scenario, which reflects current law, total spending for health care would increase to about 26 percent of GDP by 2035. (All years reported here are calendar years.) By 2080, total spending on health care under that scenario would account for roughly 41 percent of GDP, in CBO's estimation. Under the alternative fiscal scenario, in which several policies designed to restrain federal spending on health care are assumed not to continue in effect, total spending on health care as a share of GDP would be about 1 percentage point higher in 2035 and roughly 2 percentage points higher in 2080.

Methodology

To estimate total spending for health care for the 2009–2019 period, CBO started with its projections of federal spending on the government's major mandatory health care programs—Medicare, Medicaid, the Children's Health Insurance Program, and the insurance subsidies that will be provided through exchanges established by the recently enacted health care legislation (the Patient Protection and Affordable Care Act and the Health Care and Education Reconciliation Act of 2010). Other spending for health care includes payments by private health insurers, out-of- pocket payments by households, and other public spending. CBO projected those categories of spending for the 2009–2019 period using its projections of payments by private health insurers and the CMS actuaries' projections of all other components of that spending. CBO also relied on the CMS actuaries' estimate of the incremental effects of the recently enacted health care legislation on other spending (that is, spending other than federal spending on the major mandatory health care programs).[2] Through 2019, those projections show higher levels of other spending and total spending on health care as a result of the legislation.

CBO derived the path of other spending on health care after 2019 by combining its projections of demographic and economic changes with assumptions about excess cost growth for such spending (that is, growth in spending per person that exceeds the growth of GDP per person, after adjusting for changes in the population's age distribution). Specifically, CBO used the average rate of excess cost growth since 1985 for total health care spending—1.7 percentage points—as the initial rate of excess cost growth for the longer-term projections. CBO also assumed that the rate of excess cost growth for other health care spending in 2084 would be zero. In between, excess cost growth is assumed to decline linearly—that is, by the same number of fractional percentage points each year.

The resulting calculations of other spending were then combined with the projections of federal spending for the government's major mandatory health care programs to yield a rough projection of total spending on health care.

Comparison with CBO's 2009 Projections

In the *Long-Term Budget Outlook* that CBO released in June 2009, total spending on health care was projected to reach about 31 percent of GDP in 2035 and about 46 percent in 2080 under the extended- baseline scenario.[3] The corresponding figures for this year are about 5 percentage points lower than last year's projected levels. Essentially all of that difference in 2035 and the vast majority of the difference in 2080 is attributable to the use of updated data and to the technical changes CBO made in its methodology; the recently enacted health care legislation is projected to have much smaller effects on total spending for health care.

Specifically, the projections in last year's report used data from 2006 as the starting point and then applied the historical rate of excess cost growth for other spending on health care to determine the total amount of other spending through 2019 (after which cost growth was projected to slow). This year's report updated that starting point to 2008 and then used a combination of projections from CBO and the CMS actuaries to generate estimates for other spending between 2009 and 2019. Those changes resulted in a projected amount of other spending on health care in 2019 that is lower than the figure in last year's report—a difference of about 3 percent of GDP. After accounting for the increase in other spending expected to result from the recent legislation, CBO used that lower amount as the starting point for the projection of other spending beyond 2019. The projection for those years was also affected by technical changes in CBO's approach for projecting other spending on health care over the longer term.

[1] As used here, the term "total expenditures" means spending on health care services and supplies; it excludes spending on medical research, structures, and equipment.

[2] See Centers for Medicare and Medicaid Services, Office of the Actuary, memorandum on the effects of the Patient Protection and Affordable Care Act (April 22, 2010).

[3] Last year's report focused on net Medicare spending, so premiums paid by enrollees and other offsetting receipts for Medicare were included in other health care spending. The comparisons of Medicare and other health care spending between this chapter and last year's report adjust for that difference.

If, instead, excess cost growth for those programs continued to equal 2 percentage points indefinitely—or roughly the average rate observed since 1975—mandatory federal spending for health care would grow to between 11 percent and 12 percent of GDP by 2035. (Under the alternative fiscal scenario used in this chapter, that figure is 11 percent in 2035.) By 2080, the differences between the two projections would be much greater; mandatory federal spending on health care in that year is projected to be between 9 percent and 10 percent of GDP under the assumption that excess cost growth is zero, compared with projected spending of between 30 percent and 31 percent of GDP under the assumption that excess cost growth is equal to 2 percentage points indefinitely.

Trust Fund Measures

Projections of the balances in the Hospital Insurance Trust Fund offer another way to look at the financial status of Part A of Medicare. A commonly used measure is the actuarial balance—that is, the present value of revenues plus the current trust fund balance minus the present value of outlays and the desired trust fund balance (one year of outlays) at the end of a specified period.[55]

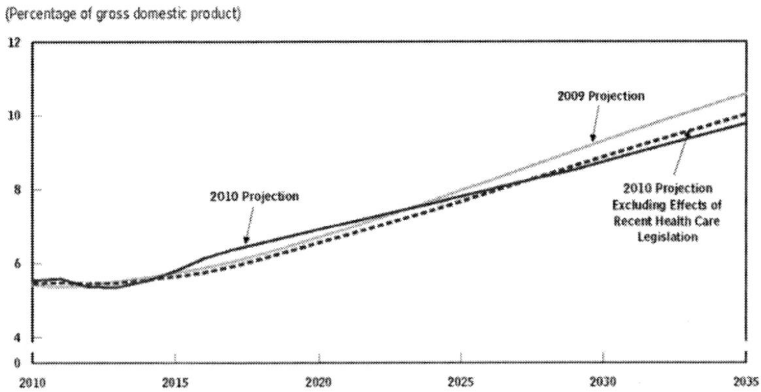

Source: Congressional Budget Office.

Note: The extended-baseline scenario adheres closely to current law, following CBO's 10-year baseline budget projections through 2020 (with adjustments for the recently enacted health care legislation) and then extending the baseline concept for the rest of the longterm projection period. (For details, see Table 1-1 on page 3.)

Figure 2.4. Comparison of CBO's 2009 and 2010 Projections of Mandatory Federal Spending on Health Care Under the Extended-Baseline Scenario.

That difference is usually shown as a percentage of the present value of taxable payroll over the same period. A negative actuarial balance means that outlays plus the desired trust fund balance will exceed revenues plus the current balance; its value represents the amount by which revenues as a percentage of taxable payroll (the income rate) would have to be increased immediately and in every year of the projection period to cover all projected costs and provide the desired balance in the trust fund at the end of the period. Alternatively, outlays as a percentage of taxable payroll (the cost rate) could be reduced by an equivalent amount—or a combination of the two approaches yielding the same total effect could be used to address the imbalance.

The recent health care legislation contains numerous provisions that will affect the actuarial balance in the HI trust fund. Many provisions will reduce outlays for Part A of Medicare. In addition, the legislation increased the HI payroll tax rate by 0.9 percentage points (to 3.8 percent) for individuals with income over $200,000 and for couples with income over $250,000 (those income thresholds are not indexed for inflation); the resulting revenues will be credited to the trust fund. (The legislation also imposes a 3.8 percent tax on investment income for the same households, but the revenues from that provision will not be directed to the HI trust fund.)

Using CBO's current projections for the extended- baseline scenario, the actuarial imbalance for the HI trust fund over 75 years is 2.4 percentage points, which is the difference between projected income equal to 4.2 percent of taxable payroll and projected costs totaling 6.5 percent of taxable payroll (see Table 2-2 on page 46). Eliminating a gap of that size would require, as an example, either an immediate increase in the basic rate of HI payroll taxes, from its current 2.9 percent to 5.3 percent, or an immediate cut of about one-third in spending on Part A. Given the tremendous uncertainty surrounding long-term projections of spending for health care, however, a more useful metric may be the actuarial imbalance in the nearer term. CBO estimates that the imbalance over 25 years is 0.7 percentage points under the extended-baseline scenario. (The projected imbalances are larger under the alternative fiscal scenario because Medicare spending is higher under that scenario and tax revenues are lower.)

In last year's report, the projected imbalances under the extended-baseline scenario were substantially larger for comparable periods—6.1 percent of taxable payroll over 75 years, and 1.3 percent over 25 years.[56] As with the projections of overall federal health care spending, differences between the current calculations of the actuarial balance and those provided last year reflect a combination of technical revisions and changes resulting from the recent legislation. (Changes in the economic forecast also affected the projections of payroll tax revenue.)

The reductions in projected Part A outlays and increases in projected HI revenues resulting from the legislation will significantly raise balances in the HI trust fund and may suggest that substantial additional resources have been set aside to pay for future Medicare benefits. However, only the additional savings by the government as a whole—from reductions in unified budget deficits— truly increase the government's ability to pay for future spending, whether for Medicare benefits or other programs. At least initially, those savings will be much smaller than the increase in balances in the trust fund. In particular, unified budget accounting shows that the majority of the HI trust fund savings achieved under the legislation through 2019 will be used to pay for other spending and therefore will not enhance the government's underlying ability to pay for future Medicare benefits. Although the HI trust fund has important legal meaning, in that its balances are a measure of the amounts that government has the legal authority to spend under current law, it has little economic significance.[57]

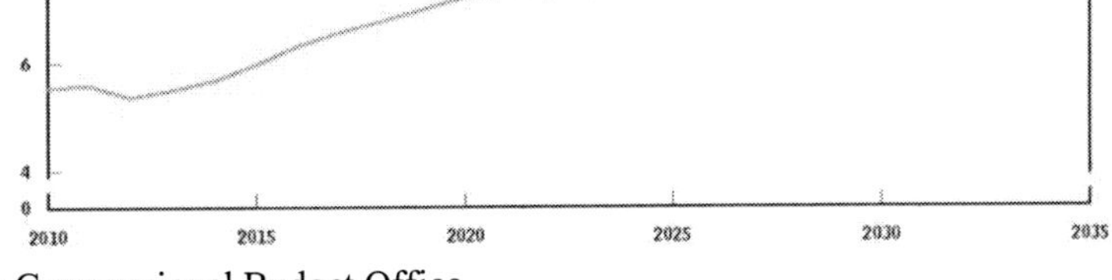

Source: Congressional Budget Office.

Notes: Excess cost growth refers to the extent to which the growth rate of annual health care spending per beneficiary is assumed to exceed the growth rate of nominal gross domestic product per capita.

The alternative fiscal scenario incorporates several changes to current law that are widely expected to occur or that would modify some provisions that might be difficult to sustain for a long period. (For details, see Table 1-1 on page 3.)

a. Under the alternative fiscal scenario, the rate of excess cost growth declines each year from an initial value of 1.7 percentage points in 2021.

Figure 2.5. Mandatory Federal Spending on Health Care Under CBO's Alternative Fiscal Scenario and Different Assumptions About Excess Cost Growth.

Table 2.2. Financial Measures for Medicare's Hospital Insurance Trust Fund Under CBO's Extended-Baseline Scenario.

(Percentage of taxable payroll)			
Projection Period (Calendar Years)	**Income Rate**	**Cost Rate**	**Actuarial Balance**
25 Years (2010 to 2034)	3.8	4.5	-0.7
50 Years (2010 to 2059)	4.0	5.5	-1.5
75 Years (2010 to 2084)	4.2	6.5	-2.4

Source: Congressional Budget Office.

Note: Over the relevant periods, the income rate is the present value of annual revenues (including the initial trust fund balance) and the cost rate is the present value of annual outlays (including the target trust fund balance at the end of the period), each divided by the present value of taxable payroll or gross domestic product. The actuarial balance is the difference between the income and cost rates.

SLOWING THE GROWTH OF HEALTH CARE COSTS

In order for policymakers to put the nation on a sustainable budgetary path, they will need to let revenues rise to much higher levels (as a share of GDP) than have been collected historically, decrease spending significantly from projected levels, or adopt some combination of those two approaches. Because health care costs will account for a significant share of the federal budget under current law, and the growth of those costs is a major contributor to the long-term fiscal pressures facing the country, policy options to restrain the growth of federal spending on health care will continue to attract considerable interest.

The recently enacted health care legislation included many provisions designed to reduce health care spending (relative to prior projections), and it will be important to monitor the effects of those provisions carefully as they are implemented. Information learned from the pilot programs and demonstrations mandated by the legislation will be particularly useful in developing and refining future policies.

More generally, making appropriate changes in financial incentives will probably be critical in developing successful policies to restrain spending growth. In many cases, the current health care system does not provide incentives for doctors, hospitals, and other providers of health care—or their patients—to control costs. Although the recent legislation took some initial steps toward modifying those incentives, more substantial changes will probably be needed to significantly lower the future trajectory of health care spending. For example, given the key role of medical technology in contributing to spending growth, slowing the growth of spending over the long term will probably require decreasing the pace of adopting new treatments and procedures or limiting the breadth of their application. Such changes need not involve explicit rationing but could occur as a result of market mechanisms or policy changes that affect the incentives to develop and use more costly treatments.

3. The Long-Term Outlook for Social Security

The federal government spends more on Social Security than it does on any other single program. Created in 1935, the program now consists of two parts: Old-Age and Survivors Insurance (OASI), which pays benefits to retired workers and to their dependents and survivors; and Disability Insurance (DI), which makes payments to disabled workers who have not reached full retirement age (the age of eligibility for full retirement benefits) and to their dependents. In all, about 53 million people currently receive Social Security benefits. The Congressional Budget Office estimates that outlays for that program in fiscal year 2010 will total about $700 billion, accounting for one-fifth of all federal spending.

During the program's first four decades, spending for Social Security increased relative to the size of the economy, reaching about 4 percent of gross domestic product in the mid-1970s. That increase was caused largely by repeated expansions of the program. Costs rose to 4.9 percent of GDP in 1983, the year that the last major piece of legislation affecting Social Security was enacted. Between 1984 and 2008, spending for Social Security fluctuated between 4.2 percent and 4.6 percent of GDP. During the recent recession, GDP contracted and Social Security outlays increased more rapidly than they would have with stable economic growth because the number of OASI and DI claimants increased as the job market deteriorated. As a result, outlays rose to 4.8 percent of GDP in 2009 (see Figure 3-1). CBO anticipates that, if the full benefits specified under current law are paid, spending for Social Security will reach 6.2 percent of GDP in 2035 and remain close to that figure in ensuing decades.

How Social Security Works

Social Security is often characterized as a retirement program because a majority of its beneficiaries—about 69 percent—are retired workers or the spouses and children of those retired workers. In general, workers qualify for retirement benefits if they are age 62 or older and have paid sufficient Social Security taxes for at least 10 years. However, Social Security also provides other types of benefits. The program pays benefits to survivors of deceased workers, who make up 12 percent of beneficiaries. In addition, workers under the full retirement age who have had to limit their employment because of a physical or mental disability can qualify for DI benefits, in many cases with a shorter employment history. Disabled workers and their spouses and children account for 19 percent of beneficiaries.[58] (Retired workers and their dependents receive 73 percent of Social Security benefits, survivors of deceased workers receive 11 percent, and disabled workers and their spouses and children receive 16 percent of benefits.)

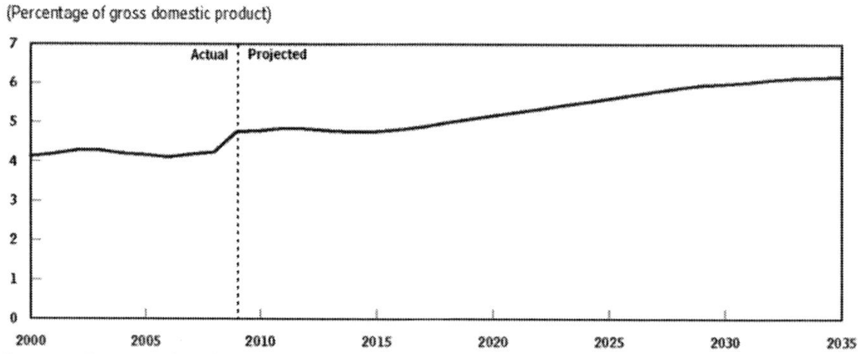

Source: Congressional Budget Office.

Note: Projected spending for Social Security is identical under CBO's two long-term budget scenarios, the extended-baseline scenario and the alternative fiscal scenario. The extended-baseline scenario adheres closely to current law, following CBO's 10-year baseline budget projections through 2020 (with adjustments for the recently enacted health care legislation) and then extending the baseline concept for the rest of the long-term projection period. The alternative fiscal scenario incorporates several changes to current law that are widely expected to occur or that would modify some provisions that might be difficult to sustain for a long period. (For details, see Table 1-1 on page 3.)

Figure 3.1. Spending for Social Security Under CBO's Long-Term Budget Scenarios.

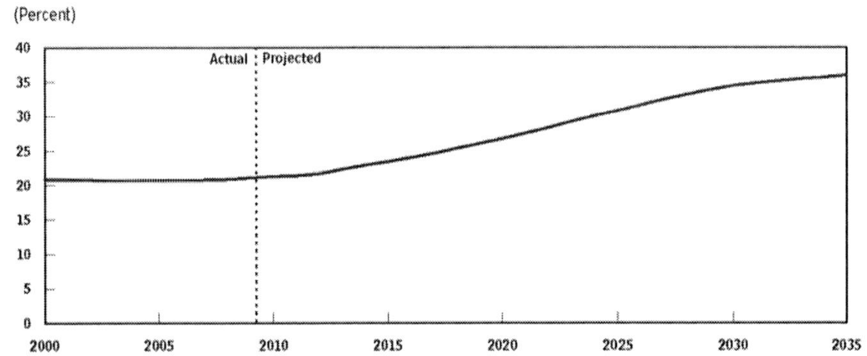

Source: Congressional Budget Office.

Figure 3.2. The Population Age 65 or Older as a Percentage of the Population Ages 20 to 64.

The benefits that retired or disabled workers initially receive are based on their individual earnings histories. Both those earnings and the formula used to compute initial benefits are indexed to changes in average annual earnings for the workforce as a whole. In subsequent years, a cost-of-living adjustment is applied to the initial benefit to reflect annual growth in consumer prices.

For workers born before 1938, the full retirement age is 65. Under current law, that age is gradually increasing and will be 67 for people born in 1960 or later. The age at which workers may start receiving reduced benefits, 62, remains the same.

The Social Security Administration estimates that workers who retire at age 65 in 2010 and who had average annual earnings—earnings equal to the average earnings of all workers in the country—throughout their career will qualify for an annual benefit of about $16,500. That amount will replace approximately 40 percent of their preretirement earnings. In coming decades, the replacement rate will be lower for workers with average earnings who retire at age 65, mainly as a result of the scheduled increase in the full retirement age. Because initial benefits are based on beneficiaries' previous earnings, indexed to overall average wages, and because wages grow over time, the real (inflation-adjusted) value of those benefits will continue to rise.

The Social Security program is funded by two sources of dedicated tax revenues. Roughly 97 percent of those revenues derive from a payroll tax—currently, 12.4 percent of earnings—that is split evenly between workers and their employers. Only earnings up to a maximum annual amount ($106,800 in 2010) are subject to the payroll tax. That amount, referred to as the taxable maximum, generally increases each year at the same rate as average earnings in the United States. The remaining share of tax revenues—3 percent—is collected from the income taxes that higher-income beneficiaries pay on their Social Security benefits. Revenues from both sources are credited to the two Social Security trust funds (the Old-Age and Survivors Insurance Trust Fund and the Disability Insurance Trust Fund). Social Security benefits and the program's administrative costs are paid from those funds; benefit payments represent roughly 99 percent of total outlays for the program. The balances currently credited to those funds have accumulated over many years, during which revenues received by the trust funds exceeded the benefit payments from those trust funds. Interest on those balances is credited to the trust funds, but because those interest transactions represent payments from one part of the government (the general fund of the Treasury) to another (the Social Security trust funds), they do not affect federal budget deficits or surpluses.

The Outlook for Social Security Spending and Revenues

The cost of the Social Security program will rise significantly in coming decades—a development that analysts have long foreseen. Average benefits per beneficiary typically grow when the economy does because the earnings on which those benefits are based also increase.[59] In addition, as members of the baby-boom generation reach retirement age, and as longer life spans lead to longer retirements, a significantly larger share of the population will draw Social Security benefits.[60] As a result, the total dollar amount of benefits scheduled to be paid under current law will grow faster than the economy.

In 2010, for the first time since the enactment of the Social Security Amendments of 1983, annual outlays for the program will exceed annual revenues, excluding interest credited to the trust funds, CBO projects. Although Social Security's revenues are likely to be greater than outlays again for the next few years, that relationship is not expected to persist. As an increasing number of baby boomers reach retirement age, outlays will increase relative to the size of the economy. As a result, by the latter part of this decade, outlays will regularly exceed revenues, excluding interest, if the benefits specified under current law are paid.

According to CBO's projections, the number of people age 65 or older will increase by 90 percent between now and 2035, compared with an increase of just 12 percent over that period in the number of people ages 20 to 64. Today, that older population is one-fifth the size of the younger population; at those rates of growth, it will be more than one-third the size of the younger group by 2035 (see Figure 3-2). About 92 million people will be collecting Social Security benefits in 2035, CBO projects, compared with 53 million who receive benefits today. Furthermore, the average benefit will have grown nearly as fast as GDP per person. CBO therefore estimates that, unless changes are made to Social Security, spending for the program will rise from 4.8 percent of GDP today to 6.2 percent by 2035. Spending for Social Security will then dip slightly to 5.9 percent as members of the large baby-boom generation die, but it will later turn upward again—reaching 6.3 percent of GDP in 2080—as a result of beneficiaries' increasing life spans.[61]

CBO's projections of outlays for Social Security are the same under both of the scenarios discussed in this chapter—the extended-baseline scenario and the alternative fiscal scenario—but projections of Social Security revenues depend upon which of those scenarios is used. The revenues generated by payroll taxes are identical under the two scenarios; however, projections of revenues derived from the taxation of Social Security benefits are higher under the extended-baseline scenario.[62] Under that scenario, which is based on the assumption that provisions of current law remain unchanged, both the number of Social Security beneficiaries subject to taxes on benefits and average income tax rates would increase.[63] As a result, income taxes on Social Security benefits would grow to 4 percent of benefits in 2016, 6 percent in 2035, and 9 percent by 2080. Under the alternative fiscal scenario, which is based on CBO's assumption that tax rates would be lower, the income taxes on Social Security benefits that are credited to the Social Security trust funds would equal 4 percent of benefits in 2020 and later, CBO projects. Consequently, the projections of Social Security's finances are somewhat less favorable under the alternative fiscal scenario than they are under the extended-baseline scenario.

A commonly used measure of the sustainability of a program that has a trust fund and a dedicated revenue source is its actuarial balance—that is, the sum of the present value of revenues and the current trust fund balance minus the sum of the present value of outlays and a target balance at the end of the period—over a specified period.[64] For Social Security, that difference is traditionally presented as a percentage of the present value of taxable payroll over the period under consideration. CBO estimates that over the next 75 years, dedicated revenues—payroll taxes and taxes on benefits—will fall short of scheduled benefits in Social Security by 1.6 percent of taxable payroll under the extended-baseline scenario (see Table 3-1). That shortfall equals 0.6 percent of GDP. In other words, to bring the program into actuarial balance over the next 75 years, payroll taxes could be immediately increased by 1.6

percent of taxable payroll and kept at that higher rate, or scheduled benefits could be reduced by an equivalent amount. Under the alternative fiscal scenario, the shortfall would be 2.1 percent of taxable payroll, or 0.8 percent of GDP.

Table 3.1. Financial Measures for Social Security Under CBO's Long-Term Budget Scenarios.

Projection Period (Calendar years)	Income Rate	Cost Rate	Actuarial Balance
	As a Percentage of Taxable Payroll		
	Extended-Baseline Scenario		
25 Years (2010 to 2034)	15.2	15.1	0.2
50 Years (2010 to 2059)	14.6	15.7	-1.2
75 Years (2010 to 2084)	14.4	16.0	-1.6
	Alternative Fiscal Scenario		
25 Years (2010 to 2034)	15.1	15.1	*
50 Years (2010 to 2059)	14.2	15.7	-1.5
75 Years (2010 to 2084)	14.0	16.0	-2.1
	As a Percentage of Gross Domestic Product		
	Extended-Baseline Scenario		
25 Years (2010 to 2034)	5.7	5.6	0.1
50 Years (2010 to 2059)	5.3	5.8	-0.4
75 Years (2010 to 2084)	5.2	5.8	-0.6
	Alternative Fiscal Scenario		
25 Years (2010 to 2034)	5.6	5.6	*
50 Years (2010 to 2059)	5.2	5.8	-0.5
75 Years (2010 to 2084)	5.1	5.9	-0.8

Source: Congressional Budget Office.

Notes: Over the relevant periods, the income rate is the present value of annual revenues (including the initial trust fund balance) and the cost rate is the present value of annual outlays (including the target trust fund balance at the end of the period), each divided by the present value of taxable payroll or gross domestic product. The actuarial balance is the difference between the income and cost rates.

The extended-baseline scenario adheres closely to current law, following CBO's 10-year baseline budget projections through 2020 (with adjustments for the recently enacted health care legislation) and then extending the baseline concept for the rest of the longterm projection period. The alternative fiscal scenario incorporates several changes to current law that are widely expected to occur or that would modify some provisions that might be difficult to sustain for a long period. (For details, see Table 1-1 on page 3.)

* = between -0.05 percent and 0.05 percent.

Another commonly used measure of the program's sustainability is the trust funds' exhaustion date, which CBO projects will be 2039 under the extended-baseline scenario and 2037 under the alternative fiscal scenario.[65] Once the trust funds are depleted, the Social Security Administration would no longer have legal authority to pay benefits. In the years following the exhaustion of the trust funds, annual outlays would therefore be limited to annual revenues. As a result, the benefits that can be paid under current law are substantially lower than the benefits that are scheduled to be paid. Thus, benefits can be projected in two ways: as "payable benefits," which reflect the limits imposed by the availability of balances in the trust funds; or as "scheduled benefits," which reflect the benefit formulas specified in law, regardless of the trust funds' balances. This chapter uses the latter approach, which is consistent with a long-standing statutory requirement that CBO, in its baseline projections, assume that laws are implemented as specified and that funding for entitlement programs is adequate to make all payments.[66]

Changes in CBO's Long-Term Social Security Projections Since June 2009

The shortfalls for Social Security that CBO is currently projecting are larger than the ones projected in last year's *Long-Term Budget Outlook*. The 75-year imbalance has increased from 1.3 percent of taxable payroll under the extended-baseline scenario to 1.6 percent and from 1.5 percent of taxable payroll under the alternative fiscal scenario to 2.1 percent. Those differences are the result of changes in both projected outlays and projected revenues. The projected 75-year cost rate—a measure of outlays— is about 2 percent higher under both scenarios, owing to near-term economic weakness, slightly lower projections of real wage growth, and technical modeling changes. The projected 75-year income rate—a measure of Social Security revenues—is about 1 percent lower than in 2009 under the alternative fiscal scenario because taxes on benefits are projected to be lower as a share of benefits. However, the projected income rate is slightly higher than in 2009 under the extended-baseline scenario because taxes on benefits are projected to be higher as a share of benefits.

Slowing the Growth of Social Security Spending

CBO has recently evaluated a number of different policy options for changing Social Security and will present the results of that analysis in a separate report. That report focuses on how the options, if implemented, would affect Social Security's finances and alter the distribution of benefits paid to and taxes paid by people in various groups distinguished by household income and year of birth.[67] Among the options considered are a variety of ways of reducing benefits and raising payroll taxes.

Three broad approaches for constraining the rise in spending for Social Security have received considerable attention. Those approaches, which could be implemented separately or in combination, are as follows:

- Reduce the size of the initial payments that new Social Security beneficiaries are scheduled to receive;
- Raise the age specified in law—currently 67 for people born in 1960 or later—at which workers become eligible for full retirement benefits (thereby reducing the amount of the initial benefit received at any specific age at which a claimant chooses to start receiving benefits); or
- Reduce the annual cost-of-living adjustment that beneficiaries receive once they become eligible for benefits.

Alternatively, or in addition, Social Security's finances could be improved by increasing the revenues flowing into the trust funds—for example, by raising the payroll tax rate or subjecting more earnings to the payroll tax. Policymakers could also restore the system to long-term actuarial balance by dedicating more general fund revenues to Social Security, but that action would have no effect on the overall federal budget.

People generally consider the size of their expected Social Security benefits when deciding how much to save for retirement and how long to work. Those benefits are a major source of income for many people, and enacting any reductions in benefits well in advance of implementation would give people time to respond by adjusting their plans for saving and retirement.

4. THE LONG-TERM OUTLOOK FOR REVENUES

Federal revenues come from a variety of sources, including individual and corporate income taxes, payroll taxes, excise taxes, estate and gift taxes, customs duties, and other taxes and fees. Currently, proceeds from individual income taxes and payroll taxes account for about 85 percent of the federal government's revenues.

Predicting the amount of revenues that will be collected in the future is difficult because such receipts are sensitive to economic developments and because policymakers frequently make changes to tax law. This analysis focuses on two sets of assumptions about future policy—the extended-baseline scenario and the alternative fiscal scenario.

The extended-baseline scenario is based on the assumption that the provisions of current law remain in effect. Thus, under this scenario, the tax cuts enacted in the Economic Growth and Tax Relief Reconciliation Act of 2001 (EGTRRA) and the Jobs and Growth Tax Relief Reconciliation Act of 2003 (JGTRRA) would expire as scheduled in 2011; the tax relief provisions in the American Recovery and Reinvestment Act of 2009 (ARRA, Public Law 111-5) would expire as scheduled in 2010 or 2011; and the exemption amounts for the individual alternative minimum tax would remain as they were at the beginning of 2010.[68] The same assumptions were incorporated in the Congressional Budget Office's March 2010 baseline projections. However, the estimates in this chapter differ from those projections because they also reflect the tax increases included in recent health care legislation—the Patient Protection and Affordable Care Act (P.L. 111-148), as amended by the Health Care and Education Reconciliation Act of 2010 (P.L. 111-152)— that was enacted after CBO's March projections were completed.

Under the extended-baseline scenario, revenues would rise considerably over time as a share of gross domestic product because of the various tax reductions that are scheduled to expire and the tax increases enacted in the health care legislation that are scheduled to go into effect. In addition, the economic recovery and the interaction of the tax system with cumulative inflation and real (inflation-adjusted) growth in income would produce higher average tax rates—that is, taxes as a share of income. As a result, revenues would rise from 15 percent of GDP in 2010 to 21 percent in 2020 and to 23 percent in 2035, for a total increase of roughly 8 percentage points over the next 25 years (see Figure 4-1). By 2035, the tax system would be quite different from what it is today. Households at all points in the income scale would pay a higher share of their income in taxes than similar households pay today and a much larger share of households— nearly half—would be subject to the AMT.[69]

The alternative fiscal scenario, by contrast, embodies several possible changes to current law that would continue certain tax policies that people have grown accustomed to—because those policies are in place now or were in place until recently. In particular, most tax cuts enacted under EGTRRA and JGTRRA, which are currently scheduled to expire in 2011, are assumed to remain in place. Those extensions would apply primarily to middle- and low-income taxpayers; certain provisions applying to high-income taxpayers (married couples with adjusted gross income above $250,000 and singles with income above $200,000) would not be extended. Also under this scenario, the tax rates and effective exemption amounts for the estate and gift tax that were in effect during 2009 (and expired at the end of that year) are assumed to be reinstated, and tax relief from the AMT is assumed to be extended. Versions of some of these changes, such as those related to the alternative minimum tax, have regularly been enacted in the past. Those and certain other changes assumed in the scenario—such as changes related to the 2001 and 2003 tax cuts—are widely expected to be made in some form over the next few years. If they are, they will receive special treatment under the new Statutory Pay-As-You-Go Act of 2010 (Public Law 111-139). (See Box 1-1 on page 4 for details.)

In constructing the alternative fiscal scenario, CBO projected revenues through 2020 on the basis of those specific policy assumptions; after 2020, the scenario is based on the assumption that tax policy would evolve over time so as to maintain total revenues at a constant share of GDP.

As a result, revenues as a share of GDP after 2020 are roughly 1 percentage point higher under the alternative fiscal scenario than the average share observed over the past 40 years. Revenues as a share of GDP have moved above or below that average between 1970 and 2010 but typically return to somewhere near the average, suggesting that changes in policy have offset other aspects of the tax system that otherwise would have tended to increase the revenue share over time In the alternative fiscal scenario, CBO assumed that those sorts of policy changes would continue.

Revenues as a share of GDP would increase from 15 percent of GDP in 2010 to just over 19 percent in 2020 and would remain constant at about 19 percent of GDP thereafter. Revenues projected under the alternative fiscal scenario are considerably lower than those estimated under the extended-baseline scenario—by about 2 percent of GDP in 2020 and by about 4 percent of GDP in 2035.

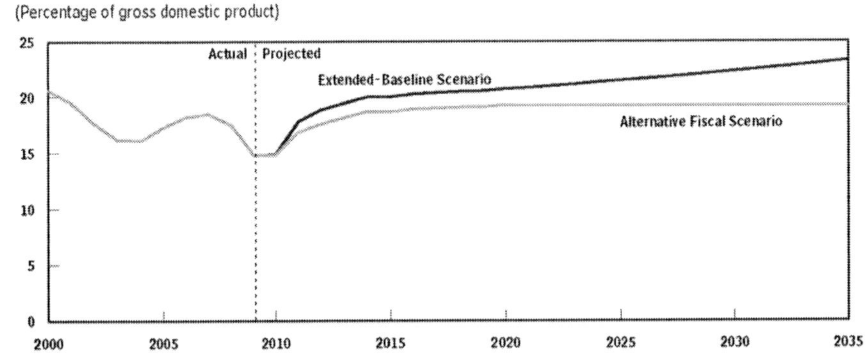

Source: Congressional Budget Office.

Note: The extended-baseline scenario adheres closely to current law, following CBO's 10-year baseline budget projections through 2020 (with adjustments for the recently enacted health care legislation) and then extending the baseline concept for the rest of the longterm projection period. The alternative fiscal scenario incorporates several changes to current law that are widely expected to occur or that would modify some provisions that might be difficult to sustain for a long period. (For details, see Table 4-1.)

Figure 4.1. Total Revenues Under CBO's Long-Term Budget Scenarios.

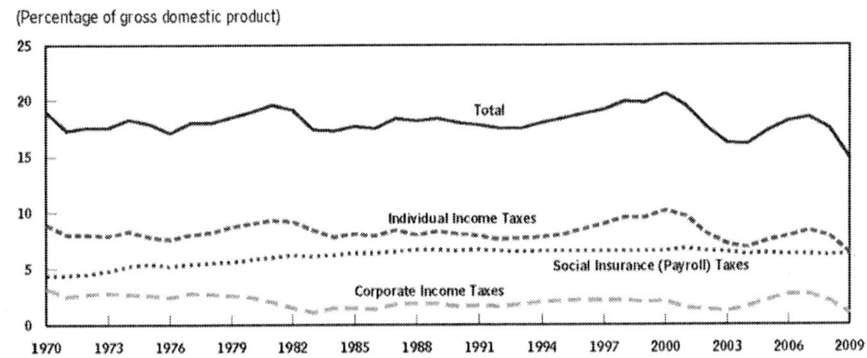

Source: Congressional Budget Office.

Figure 4.2. Revenues, by Source, 1970 to 2009.

Revenues Over the Past 40 Years

Over the past 40 years, total federal revenues have ranged from 14.8 percent to 20.6 percent of GDP, averaging 18.1 percent, with no evident trend over time (see Figure 4-2). During that period, however, the various sources of revenue have changed in importance. Individid- ual income taxes, which account for about half of all revenues now, have varied between about 6 percent and 10 percent of GDP. Social insurance taxes, which generate about one-third of total revenues now, have grown from 4 percent to over 6 percent of GDP. (Those taxes consist primarily of payroll taxes credited to the Social Security and Medicare Hospital Insurance Trust Funds.) Corporate income taxes contribute less now than they did in earlier years: In 2009, they represented about 1 percent of GDP, down from 3 percent in 1970. Revenues from other sources have varied between roughly 1 percent and 3 percent of GDP over the past 40 years.

Table 4.1. Assumptions About Revenues Underlying CBO's Long-Term Budget Scenarios.

	Extended-Baseline Scenario	**Alternative Fiscal Scenario**
Individual Income Taxes	As scheduled under current law	Through 2020, tax cuts from EGTRRA and JGTRRA are extended (except for rate reductions that apply to high-income taxpayers) and AMT relief is extended; thereafter, individual income taxes are adjusted to keep total revenues constant as a share of GDPa
Payroll Taxes	As scheduled under current law	As scheduled under current law
Corporate Income Taxes	As scheduled under current law through 2020; remaining constant as a share of GDP thereafter	As scheduled under current law through 2020; remaining constant as a share of GDP thereafter
Excise Taxes	As scheduled under current law	As scheduled under current law through 2020; remaining constant as a share of GDP thereafter
Estate and Gift Taxes	As scheduled under current law	2009 tax rates and exemption amount (adjusted for inflation) continue through 2020; revenues are constant as a share of GDP thereaftera

Table 4.1. (Continued)

	Extended-Baseline Scenario	Alternative Fiscal Scenario
Other Sources of Revenue	As scheduled under current law through 2020; remaining constant as a share of GDP thereafter	As scheduled under current law through 2020; remaining constant as a share of GDP thereafter

Source: Congressional Budget Office.

Notes: The extended-baseline scenario adheres closely to current law, following CBO's 10-year baseline budget projections through 2020 (with adjustments for the recently enacted health care legislation) and then extending the baseline concept for the rest of the longterm projection period. The alternative fiscal scenario incorporates several changes to current law that are widely expected to occur or that would modify some provisions that might be difficult to sustain for a long period. For details, see Table 1-1.

EGTRRA = Economic Growth and Tax Relief Reconciliation Act of 2001; JGTRRA = Jobs and Growth Tax Relief Reconciliation Act of 2003; AMT = alternative minimum tax; GDP = gross domestic product.

[a] These assumptions are consistent with extending through 2020 provisions that are the basis for "current-policy" adjustments specified in the Statutory Pay-As-You-Go Act of 2010—with the exception that the alternative fiscal scenario assumes that all of the policies would continue through 2020, whereas the act's "current-policy" adjustments for the estate tax parameters and the AMT end after 2011 (see Box 1-1 on page 4).

Some of the variation in the composition of total tax revenues has stemmed from the interaction between the tax code and changes in the economy. For example, many excise taxes are levied on the quantity of a good purchased (for instance, cents per gallon of gasoline) as opposed to a percentage of the price paid. Because those levies are not indexed for inflation, revenues derived from excise taxes have diminished in magnitude relative to GDP as the general level of prices has risen. In contrast, in the absence of legislative reductions to individual income taxes, receipts from individual income taxes have tended to grow relative to GDP. That increase has occurred because rising income tends to push people into higher tax brackets. Before 1984, when none of the parameters of the individual income tax were indexed for inflation, inflation by itself caused an increase in revenues as a greater share of income was taxed at higher rates.[70] Even after 1984, when many of the parameters of the tax system were first indexed for inflation, growth in real income has caused a greater share of income to be taxed at higher rates (and not all of the parameters of the tax system are indexed for inflation, so rising prices have continued to have some effect).

Tax revenues as a share of GDP have also varied over time as a result of legislative changes. In the past 40 years, lawmakers have enacted at least a dozen pieces of legislation that have raised or lowered revenues by at least 0.5 percent of GDP per year.

Revenue Projections Under CBO's Long-Term Budget Scenarios

The extended-baseline scenario and the alternative fiscal scenario embody two possible paths for revenues over future decades. CBO's assumptions about particular revenue sources under the two scenarios are summarized in Table 4-1.

Table 4.2. Sources of Growth in Total Revenues as a Share of GDP Between 2010 and 2035 Under CBO's Extended-Baseline Scenario.

Source of Growth	Percentage of GDP
Impact of Economic Recovery on Individual Income Taxes	0.6
Expiring Individual Income Tax Provisions and the AMT	2.7
Other Structural Features of the Tax System (Including real bracket creep)	2.6
Demographic Trends	0.5
Health Care Legislation	1.2
Other Factors (Including corporate, excise, and estate and gift taxes)	0.8
Total Growth in Revenues as a Share of GDP	**8.4**

Notes: The extended-baseline scenario adheres closely to current law, following CBO's 10-year baseline budget projections through 2020 (with adjustments for the recently enacted health care legislation) and then extending the baseline concept for the rest of the longterm projection period. The alternative fiscal scenario incorporates several changes to current law that are widely expected to occur or that would modify some provisions that might be difficult to sustain for a long period. (For details, see Table 4-1.)

"Real bracket creep" refers to the phenomenon in which rising real (inflation-adjusted) income causes an ever-larger proportion of income to be subject to higher tax brackets.

GDP = gross domestic product; AMT = alternative minimum tax.

The Extended-Baseline Scenario

The extended-baseline scenario follows current law. That scenario uses the 10-year baseline projections for revenues that CBO published in March 2010, after incorporating the estimated effects of the recently enacted health care legislation (which are unchanged from the estimates CBO released in March). As was the case with the March baseline, the scenario is based on the assumption that certain tax provisions will expire as scheduled and new provisions of law will go into effect as scheduled. The specific assumptions are the following:

- The tax provisions of the Economic Growth and Tax Relief Reconciliation Act of 2001, the Jobs and Growth Tax Relief Reconciliation Act of 2003, and the American Recovery and Reinvestment Act of 2009 will expire as scheduled;
- The AMT exemption amounts in effect at the beginning of 2010 will remain at those levels, and the parameters of the AMT will not be indexed for inflation; and
- Tax increases scheduled to go into effect in future years as a result of recently enacted health care legislation will be implemented as specified in current law. Such increases include the new taxes on earnings and investment income (beginning in 2013) and the new tax on employment-based health insurance plans with high premiums (beginning in 2018).

Under the extended-baseline scenario, current law would remain in place indefinitely after 2020, extending those baseline assumptions for the rest of the long-term projection period.

Under those assumptions, tax revenues would sharply increase in the next few years and then steadily rise thereafter relative to GDP. The individual income tax system will be responsible for much of the increase in the ratio of total revenues to GDP because of the various ways in which its structure interacts with the economy. Under the extended-baseline scenario, individual income tax receipts would rise by about 6.5 percentage points of GDP between 2010 and 2035 and by a smaller amount over the remainder of the long-term forecast horizon. That increase in individual income tax revenues reflects a number of factors, including the anticipated economic recovery; the expiration of tax-relief provisions in EGTRRA and JGTRRA; the growing impact of the AMT; other structural features of the income tax system; and demographic trends. Total revenues will also increase relative to GDP because of additional revenues from other tax sources as a result of the recent health care legislation, the reinstatement of the estate tax after 2010, and certain other factors.

Economic Recovery

CBO projects that revenues will grow faster than GDP in 2011 and 2012 as the economy continues to recover, with most of that growth coming from individual income taxes. Certain sources of income that had been unusually low during the downturn (for instance, capital gains realizations) are expected to recover and return to levels consistent with an economy slowly moving closer to its long-term growth path. The effects of the recovery will increase revenues from individual income taxes as a share of GDP by 0.6 percentage points, CBO estimates (see Table 4-2).

Expiring Tax Provisions and the AMT

Certain aspects of current tax law will also cause an increase in individual income tax revenues relative to GDP. Most of the provisions in EGTRRA and JGTRRA are scheduled to expire after December 31, 2010, as are most of the tax provisions in ARRA. When that happens, certain features of the tax code will revert to prior law: Tax rates will rise, the value of some tax credits will decrease, other credits will expire, and thresholds for certain tax rates will change. Those changes will increase receipts as a share of GDP in 2011 and beyond.

Another factor that will increase revenues relative to GDP is the growing impact of the AMT. The alternative minimum tax is a parallel individual income tax system that provides fewer exemptions, deductions, and rates than the regular income tax. Households must calculate the amount they owe under both the AMT and the regular income tax and then pay the higher of the two amounts.[71] The parameters that determine the amount owed under the AMT are not indexed for inflation. Therefore, as inflation increases people's income over time, more taxpayers will be subject to the AMT and that tax will claim a larger share of GDP.

The effects of the expiration of EGTRRA and JGTRRA and of the growing reach of the AMT can be identified by comparing CBO's projection of individual income tax revenues under the extended-baseline scenario, which follows current law, with two alternatives. The first is based on the assumption that policymakers would deviate from current law by permanently extending the tax provisions of EGTRRA and JGTRRA but would not index the AMT for inflation; the second reflects the assumption that policymakers would extend those tax provisions and also index the AMT.

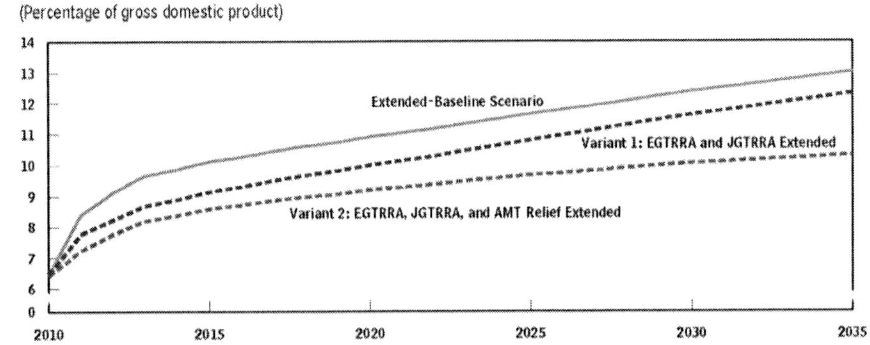

Source: Congressional Budget Office.

Notes: The extended-baseline scenario adheres closely to current law, following CBO's 10-year baseline budget projections through 2020 (with adjustments for the recently enacted health care legislation) and then extending the baseline concept for the rest of the longterm projection period. (For details, see Table 4-1.) EGTRRA = Economic Growth and Tax Relief Reconciliation Act of 2001; JGTRRA = Jobs and Growth Tax Relief Reconciliation Act of 2003; AMT = alternative minimum tax.

Figure 4.3. Individual Income Tax Revenues Under CBO's Extended-Baseline Scenario and Two Variants.

Relative to the extended-baseline scenario, extending EGTRRA and JGTRRA alone would lower individual income tax revenues—and thus total revenues—by 0.9 percent of GDP in 2012 and by 0.7 percent in 2035 (see Figure 4-3). That decline in revenues as a share of GDP would lessen over time because of the growth of the AMT. As a greater share of individual income taxes was paid through the AMT, the effect of extending EGTRRA and JGTRRA would decline because many of the provisions of those laws do not benefit taxpayers who are subject to the AMT.

Relative to the extended-baseline scenario, extending the provisions of EGTRRA and JGTRRA and indexing the AMT for inflation would lower revenues from individual income taxes (and total revenues) by 1.4 percent of GDP in 2012 and by 2.7 percent in 2035. That effect would increase over time as cumulative inflation caused more taxpayers to be subject to the AMT.

Other Structural Features of the Income Tax System

Even if the AMT was indexed for inflation and the tax provisions of EGTRRA and JGTRRA were made permanent, individual income tax revenues would continue to rise as a percentage of GDP. Most of the parameters of the individual income tax apart from the AMT are indexed for inflation, which prevents average tax rates from rising when incomes are increasing only with inflation. Rising real incomes, however, cause an ever-larger proportion of income to be subject to higher tax rates, a phenomenon known as "real bracket creep." Rising real incomes also increase taxes by reducing taxpayers' eligibility for various credits, such as the earned income tax credit and the child tax credit. In addition, some provisions of the tax code are not indexed for inflation, so cumulative inflation would generate some increase in receipts relative to GDP. All told, even if the AMT was indexed and the expiring tax provisions were extended, growth in people's nominal income would increase income tax revenues relative to GDP by 2.6 percentage points between 2010 and 2035, CBO estimates.

Demographic Trends

Over the next few decades, another factor will cause income tax revenues to increase as a share of GDP: the retirement of members of the baby-boom generation. Although certain contributions to retirement plans—such as 401(k) plans and individual retirement accounts—are tax-exempt when they are made, and the income earned on assets in those accounts is also exempt from taxes, withdrawals from plans with deductible contributions are subject to taxation.[72] Likewise, compensation that is deferred under employer-sponsored definedbenefit plans is not taxed when it is earned. As baby boomers withdraw money from retirement accounts and receive pension benefits, those sums will make up a rising portion of taxable income. Thus, the Treasury will receive significant tax revenues that have essentially been deferred for years, which will tend to boost tax receipts relative to GDP. As a result, under the extended-baseline scenario, projected revenues as a share of GDP would climb by about 0.5 percentage points between 2010 and 2035. That upward trend would end in the mid-2030s, so beyond that point, revenues from taxable withdrawals would no longer grow faster than GDP.

Effects of Recent Health Care Legislation

One key provision of the legislation is an excise tax on high- premium health insurance plans. Under that provision, employment-based plans with premiums exceeding a specified threshold will generally be subject to an excise tax of 40 percent. That tax, which will be levied on insurers but most likely passed on to their customers, will increase revenues in two ways. First, in those cases in which the tax applies, it will generate additional excise tax revenues. Second, many individuals and employers will probably respond to the presence of the excise tax by shifting to lower-cost insurance plans—plans with premiums below the tax threshold—to avoid paying the excise tax. As a result, total payments of health insurance premiums for those individuals will be less than they would have been in the absence of the tax. Because, over the long term, total compensation paid by employers would not be affected, lower expenditures for health insurance would mean higher taxable wages for employees and, as a result, higher payments for income and payroll taxes.

Although the threshold for the tax on high-premium health insurance plans is indexed for changes in overall consumer prices, health care costs will grow faster than prices over the long term, CBO projects and, consequently, a greater share of premiums will be subject to the excise tax.[73] Thus, in CBO's estimation, whether policyholders pay the excise tax through higher premiums or avoid it by switching to lower-cost plans, total taxes will ultimately rise in comparison with what would have happened in the absence of the new excise tax. Accordingly, CBO projects that the excise tax will increase revenues by just over 0.5 percent of GDP in 2035 and eventually by over 3 percent of GDP in 2080. Because health care spending so far into the future is highly uncertain, projections at that horizon of the revenue loss from rising health care costs and the revenue gain from the excise tax are particularly uncertain.[74]

Other provisions of the new health care legislation that will boost revenues as a share of GDP are additional taxes on earnings and on investment income, which will be assessed on individuals with income in excess of $200,000 and on families with income in excess of $250,000. Those thresholds are not indexed for inflation. Because an increasing share of earnings and investment income will become subject to the new surtaxes over time, CBO projects that the new levies will increase revenues by a small but growing share of GDP over time. Other provisions of the health care legislation will also raise revenues by small amounts as a share of GDP.

Under the extended-baseline scenario, CBO estimates, the recent health care legislation would raise revenues as a share of GDP by 0.5 percent in 2020, by 1.2 percent in 2035, and by increasing amounts thereafter. Increases in revenues from the recent legislation would offset a decline in revenues from rising health care costs. In CBO's estimation, those costs would cause a growing portion of workers' compensation to be paid as nontaxable health insurance benefits, holding down both income and payroll tax revenues.

Other Factors Affecting Revenue Projections

In addition to the factors already discussed, other factors would also affect the growth of federal revenues as a share of GDP under the extended-baseline scenario. According to CBO's projections, corporate income tax revenues are expected to rise as a share of GDP over the next 10 years, reflecting an anticipated rebound from a historically low share of GDP in 2010 as the economy recovers from the recession. Estate and gift taxes are projected to increase as a share of GDP following the reinstatement of the estate tax after 2010. The dollar amount of an estate that is exempt from taxation will remain fixed at $1 million starting in 2011 and not be indexed for inflation thereafter; as a result, a greater share of wealth would become subject to the tax over time. Excluding the new excise tax on high-premium health insurance plans, excise taxes are projected to decline slightly as a share of GDP over time because many excise taxes are assessed as a fixed dollar amount per quantity of a good that is purchased and not as a percentage of the price paid for that good. Therefore, as the general price level rises over time, excise taxes tend to fall as a share of GDP. On balance, CBO projects that in the absence of the excise tax on high-premium health insurance plans, revenue derived from corporate income taxes, estate and gift taxes, federal excise taxes, and other miscellaneous receipts will rise by 0.8 percent of GDP between 2010 and 2035 and by a small amount after 2035.

The Alternative Fiscal Scenario

The alternative fiscal scenario is based on the assumption that certain tax policies that have recently expired, or that are scheduled to expire, will be extended through 2020, and that tax policies will adjust so that revenues remain at a constant share of GDP thereafter. Specifically:

- Certain provisions of EGTRRA and JGTRRA are assumed to be extended, including the $1,000 child tax credit, marriage penalty relief, and lower tax rates for taxpayers with incomes under $250,000;
- AMT relief, which expired at the end of 2009, is assumed to be extended; and
- The estate tax, which expired completely in 2010 and is scheduled to be reinstated in 2011—at the rates and exemption amounts scheduled to apply in 2011 before the law was changed in 2001—is assumed instead to be extended at the rates in effect in 2009 and with the exemption amounts (adjusted for inflation) that applied in that year.

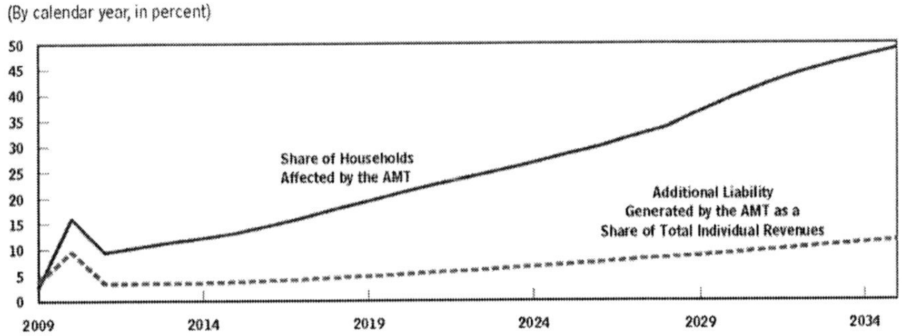

Source: Congressional Budget Office.

Notes: The shares of households and revenues rise in 2010 after the temporary increase in the AMT exemption expires. After 2010, the shares initially fall because taxes and the regular income tax rise with the expiration of certain provisions of the Economic Growth and Tax Relief Reconciliation Act of 2001 and the Jobs and Growth Tax Relief Reconciliation Act of 2003.

The extended-baseline scenario adheres closely to current law, following CBO's 10-year baseline budget projections through 2020 (with adjustments for the recently enacted health care legislation) and then extending the baseline concept for the rest of the longterm projection period. (For details, see Table 4-1.)

AMT = alternative minimum tax.

Figure 4.4. The Impact of the Alternative Minimum Tax on Individual Income Tax Liability Under CBO's Extended-Baseline Scenario, 2009 to 2035.

Those changes are widely expected to be made in some form over the next few years. If they are, they will receive special treatment under the new Statutory Pay-As-YouGo Act of 2010. Under those assumptions, the growth in revenues between 2010 and 2020 would amount to about 4 percentage points, from 15 percent of GDP to just over 19 percent of GDP—as compared with the 6 percentage-point increase projected under the extended-baseline scenario. That projected growth in receipts is largely attributable to several factors that also matter in the extended-baseline scenario: the anticipated economic recovery over the next few years; the increase in tax rates that would affect people in the highest income brackets beginning in 2011; and the rise in estate, gift, and corporate taxes.

In the alternative fiscal scenario, CBO assumed that after 2020 a series of changes in the tax code would be enacted to offset certain factors that under the baseline scenario would increase revenues over time; as a result, revenues as a share of GDP would remain constant. The chief features of the current tax system that would cause revenues to rise are real bracket creep, unindexed tax parameters, an increase in taxable withdrawals from retirement accounts, and the long-run interaction of rising health care expenditures and health care legislation. During the past 40 years, legislative changes have kept total revenues between 15 percent and 21 percent of GDP, averaging 18.1 percent of GDP over the period. Under this scenario, revenues would remain at about 19 percent of GDP in 2035, about 4 percentage points less than is projected under the extended-baseline scenario. Revenues would remain at about 19 percent of GDP through 2080 under the alternative fiscal scenario, in contrast with their continued rise after 2035 under the extended-baseline scenario.

Changes in CBO 's Long-Term Revenue rojections Since June 2009

Compared with last year's estimates, the major change in CBO's projection of revenues this year under the extended-baseline scenario results from enactment of the health care legislation. The Patient Protection and Affordable Care Act, enacted in March 2010 and modified by the Health Care and Education Reconciliation Act, includes a number of provisions that affect revenues. Most notable among those are additional taxes on earnings and investment income that will be imposed starting in 2013 and the excise tax on high-premium health insurance plans that will go into effect in 2018. Those laws also impose new annual fees on health insurance providers and on certain manufacturers and importers of certain drugs. Altogether, CBO and the staff of the Joint Committee on Taxation estimated that the legislation would raise revenues by 0.5 percent of GDP in 2020 (as compared with what would be the case in the absence of that legislation).[75] Under the extended-baseline scenario, the impact of the legislation on the revenue share of GDP would rise over time, CBO estimates, boosting revenues by about 1.2 percent of GDP in 2035 and by a larger amount after 2035; most of the increase that is projected to occur after 2035 is attributable to the excise tax on high-premium health insurance plans.

Excluding the effects of health care legislation, CBO's current long-term projection of revenues as a share of GDP under the extended-baseline scenario is close to its 2009 projection. On net, excluding the impact of that legislation, projected federal revenues under the scenario are 0.2 percentage points lower in 2020 and 0.4 percentage points higher in 2035; after 2035, the difference diminishes. The impact of changes in the long-term economic forecast on projected individual income taxes accounts for most of the change in 2035. Cumulative inflation is slightly higher by 2035 than was projected last year, which has the effect of increasing income tax revenues relative to GDP. After 2035, cumulative inflation remains slightly higher than was projected last year, but cumulative real income growth is projected to be slightly lower; the effects of those revisions on revenues are essentially offset after 2035.

In projecting the alternative fiscal scenario for this chapter, CBO departed somewhat from the method used for its June 2009 report. First, rather than basing the scenario on the assumption that individual income tax law in effect in 2009 would be extended permanently, CBO assumed that a narrower set of policies would be continued in 2010 and beyond. Those policies are consistent with the extension through 2020 of provisions that are the basis for "current-policy" adjustments specified in the Statutory Pay-As-You-Go Act.[76] Second, and more significant over the longer term, CBO assumed in last year's report that policies in effect in 2009 would remain permanently in place after 2020, whereas the assumption this year is that revenues (including those resulting from the recently enacted health care legislation) would remain constant as a share of GDP after 2020. CBO did not specify the changes in law that would achieve a constant share of GDP after 2020. Excluding the effects of the recently enacted health care legislation, the current projections of revenues as a share of GDP under the alternative fiscal scenario are 0.2 percentage points higher in 2020 and 0.4 percentage points lower in 2035 than last year. The difference increases considerably after 2035 because of the assumption in this year's report that revenues remain constant as a share of GDP after 2020.

Implications of the Long-Term Revenue Scenarios

The tax systems that would be in place under the two scenarios would differ, in a variety of ways, from the current system. Under the extended-baseline scenario, inflation and income growth over many years would significantly change the characteristics of the tax system: Many more taxpayers would pay the AMT, marginal and average tax rates would rise, and the dollar value of some tax parameters would fall sharply in real terms and even more sharply relative to income. Changes to the tax system stemming from the expiration of EGTRRA and JGTRRA would also boost tax rates. As a result of all of those changes, people at various points in the income scale would pay a very different percentage of their income in taxes than people at the same points pay today.

Under the alternative fiscal scenario, CBO assumed that unspecified policy adjustments would be made after 2020 to keep revenues constant as a share of GDP. A wide range of policy alternatives could result in that outcome, and the specific choices that might be made would have very different implications for the economy and for the share of income paid in taxes by people at various income levels.

Impact of the AMT

If the parameters of the AMT remain unchanged, as CBO assumed in the extended-baseline scenario, the alternative minimum tax would ultimately affect a significant share of taxpayers. Just 3 percent of households were affected by the AMT in 2009—the most recent year in which temporary higher exemption amounts were in effect. However, by 2011—with the expiration of AMT relief at the end of 2009 and the expiration at the end of 2010 of the income tax cuts enacted in EGTRRA and JGTRRA—the AMT would affect 9 percent of households, CBO projects. By 2035, nearly half of the nation's households would be subject to the AMT. The AMT would also account for an increasing share of individual income tax liability over time. By 2035, roughly 12 percent of individual income tax liability would be attributable to the AMT, compared with less than 4 percent in both 2009 and 2011 (see Figure 4-4). Because taxpayers' liability under the AMT is calculated as the excess amount over the regular tax owed, the AMT's contribution to receipts is smaller than its contribution to the share of people affected by the tax.

Table 4.3. Estimates of Effective Marginal Tax Rates Under CBO's Extended- Baseline Scenario.

(Percent)	2010	2025	2035
Marginal Tax Rate on Labor Income	29	35	38
Marginal Tax Rate on Capital Income	13	16	16

Source: Congressional Budget Office.

Notes: The effective federal marginal tax rate on income from labor is the share of the last dollar of earnings in the economy that is taken by federal individual income and payroll taxes. The effective federal marginal tax rate on income from capital is the share of the last dollar of such income that is taken by federal individual and corporate income taxes.

The extended-baseline scenario adheres closely to current law, following CBO's 10-year baseline budget projections through 2020 (with adjustments for the recently enacted health care legislation) and then extending the baseline concept for the rest of the long-term projection period. (For details, see Table 4-1.)

Under the extended-baseline scenario, both the share of households subject to the AMT and the share of total revenues attributable to it would continue to rise after 2035. Sometime around 2060, revenues generated by the AMT would level off as a share of GDP as real bracket creep caused a greater share of income to be subject to the top marginal rate under the regular income tax (whereas less bracket creep would occur under the AMT because most of the income under the AMT will be taxed at the top AMT rate by then). Therefore, the amount of additional tax liability under the AMT would decline as the amount of tax calculated under the regular tax rose. The AMT would continue to apply to many taxpayers, but the additional revenue attributable to it would diminish relative to GDP.

Marginal Tax Rates on Income from Labor and Capital

Marginal tax rates on income from labor and capital would rise considerably under the extended-baseline scenario. The increase in the marginal tax rate on labor would reduce people's incentive to work, and the increase in the marginal tax rate on capital would reduce their incentive to save. However, the reduction in earnings and savings from higher taxes would create an incentive to work and save more, if people wished to maintain the same amount of after-tax income and savings. On net, evidence suggests that the former effects typically prevail and thus that higher marginal tax rates would tend to discourage some economic activity. The effect of taxes on the future path of economic output would depend not only on those marginal tax rates but also on future budget deficits and the amount of debt the government holds relative to the size of the economy.

CBO estimates that under the extended-baseline scenario, the marginal tax rate on labor income would increase by about 6 percentage points between now and 2025, and by an additional 3 percentage points between 2025 and 2035 (see Table 4-3). The increase between 2010 and 2025 includes the effects of the expiration of EGTRRA and JGTRRA after 2010, the introduction of the additional tax on earnings over $250,000 that begins in 2013, and the impact of the excise tax on certain high- premium health insurance plans that takes effect in 2018. Marginal rates on labor would also rise between 2010 and 2025 and continue to rise between 2025 and 2035 because of real bracket creep under the regular tax, the effects of the AMT on a rising number of taxpayers, and the growing impact of both the additional tax on earnings and the excise tax on certain high-premium health insurance plans.[77]

Because of the expiration of certain provisions of EGTRRA and JGTRRA, as well as the introduction of the additional tax on investment income in excess of $250,000, the marginal tax rate on capital under the extended-baseline scenario would rise by 3 percentage points between 2010 and 2025. Marginal rates on capital would remain roughly the same between 2025 and 2035 because the impact of real bracket creep and the expanding effects of the AMT would have little effect on the tax rate on capital income. (The reason is that after 2025, a large share of capital income would already be taxed at the top rate.)

In constructing the alternative fiscal scenario, CBO did not make assumptions about any specific revenue policies after 2020. The marginal tax rates on capital and labor would depend on the specific policies chosen to maintain revenues at a constant share of GDP. Therefore, CBO could not analyze marginal tax rates under the alternative fiscal scenario.

Average Tax Rates on Typical Households

Over the coming decades, the cumulative effect of rising prices will sharply reduce the value of some parameters of the tax system that are not indexed for inflation. Under the extended-baseline scenario, the estate tax exemption, which will be $1 million in 2011 under current law, would be worth about $600,000 (in 2010 dollars) by 2035; the same is true for the amount of mortgage debt eligible for the mortgage interest deduction, which is also limited to $1 million in 2011 under current law. The portion of Social Security benefits subject to taxation would increase from about 30 percent now to about 50 percent by 2035, because the thresholds for taxing benefits are fixed in nominal terms.

Even tax parameters that are indexed for inflation would lose value relative to income over the long term. The current $3,650 personal exemption would rise by almost 70 percent by 2035 because it is indexed for inflation, but income per household is projected to more than double during that period, so the value of the exemption relative to income would decline by about 30 percent.

Without legislative changes, the proportion of taxpayers claiming the earned income tax credit would fall from 15 percent this year to 10 percent in 2035 as growth in real income moved more taxpayers out of the eligibility range for the credit.

The fact that most tax parameters are not indexed for real income growth and that some are not even indexed for inflation has significant implications over the long term. Under current rules for indexing tax parameters, individual income taxes as a share of income would grow by varying amounts for households at different points in the income scale. For example, a couple with two children, earning the median income of $94,900 in 2010 and filing a joint tax return, would pay about 3 percent of their income in individual income taxes under the extended- baseline scenario (see Table 4-4).[78] By 2035, under existing tax law, a similar couple with median income would pay 13 percent of their income in individual income taxes, an increase of 10 percentage points. By comparison, if the same couple earned four times the median income, the share of income that they would pay in individual income taxes would rise from 21 percent in 2010 to 24 percent by 2035, an increase of 3 percentage points. After 2035, income taxes as a share of income would continue rising at both income levels—but again, by a greater proportion for the couple earning the median income. Taxes as a share of income for households at various other points in the income distribution would also be very different than they are today.

Table 4.4. Individual Income and Payroll Taxes as a Share of Income Under CBO's Extended-Baseline Scenario.

	Income (2010 dollars)	Taxes as a Share of Income Under the Extended-Baseline Scenario (Percent)	
		Income Taxes	Income and Payroll Taxes
	Taxpayer Filing a Single Return		
Half the Median Income			
2010	16,700	-2	8
2035	25,500	4	13
Median Income			
2010	33,400	5	18
2035	51,000	8	20
Twice the Median Income			
2010	66,800	9	22
2035	102,100	14	27
Four Times the Median Income			
2010	133,600	14	27
2035	204,300	21	33
	Married Couple with Two Children Filing a Joint Return[a]		
Half the Median Income			
2010	47,400	-11	-1

Table 4.4. (Continued)

	Income (2010 dollars)	Taxes as a Share of Income Under the Extended-Baseline Scenario (Percent)	
		Income Taxes	Income and Payroll Taxes
2035	72,600	4	14
Median Income			
2010	94,900	3	15
2035	145,200	13	25
Twice the Median Income			
2010	189,700	13	23
2035	290,300	20	30
Four Times the Median Income			
2010	379,400	21	27
2035	580,700	24	30

Source: Congressional Budget Office based on data from the March 2009 Current Population Survey.

Notes: All income is assumed to be from compensation, which includes employment-based health insurance and the employer's share of payroll taxes. For 2035, the premium on employment-based health insurance is assumed to not exceed the excise tax threshold set forth in the Patient Protection and Affordable Care Act (Public Law 111-148), as amended by the Health Care and Education Reconciliation Act of 2010 (P.L. 111-152).

Taxpayers are assumed to itemize if implied itemized deductions are greater than the standard deduction. State and local taxes are assumed to be 8 percent of wages; other deductions are assumed to be 14 percent of wages.

The extended-baseline scenario adheres closely to current law, following CBO's 10-year baseline budget projections through 2020 (with adjustments for the recently enacted health care legislation) and then extending the baseline concept for the rest of the longterm projection period. (For details, see Table 4-1.)

[a] The examples for the married couple assume that only one spouse earns income.

Despite rising average tax rates, households in the future would have higher after-tax income than similar households at the same point in the income distribution have today because of growth in real income. For example, by 2035 under the extended-baseline scenario, real after-tax income for the couple earning the median income would have grown by 35 percent since 2010, despite the increase in taxes as a share of income. The growth in pretax income would more than offset the increase in taxes.

APPENDIX A. LONG-TERM PROJECTIONS THROUGH 2080

This appendix presents longer-term versions of several figures that appear in Chapters 1, 3, and 4 of this chapter. The longer-term figures show the Congressional Budget Office's projections of categories of primary (noninterest) spending, total revenues, and debt held by the public through 2080 under the extended-baseline and alternative fiscal scenarios.

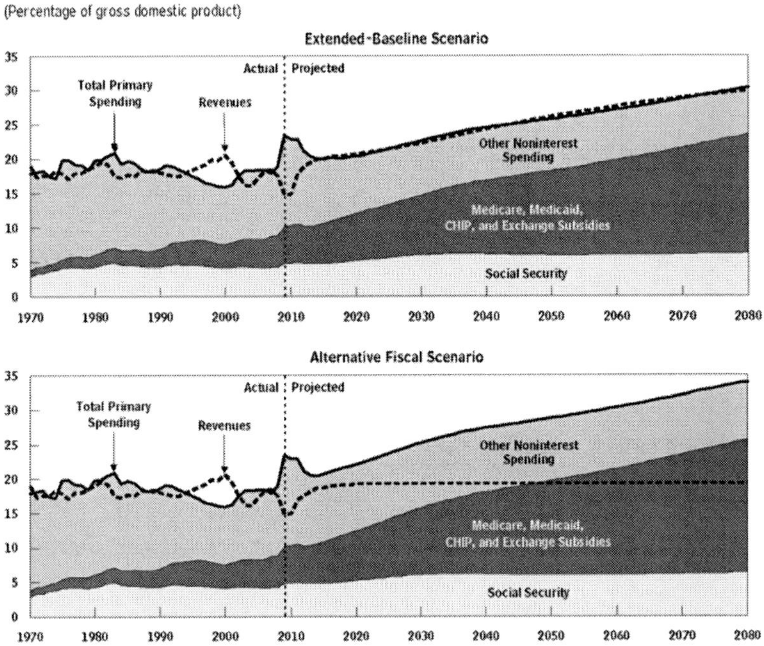

Source: Congressional Budget Office.

Notes: Primary spending refers to all spending other than interest payments on federal debt.

The extended-baseline scenario adheres closely to current law, following CBO's 10-year baseline budget projections through 2020 (with adjustments for the recently enacted health care legislation) and then extending the baseline concept for the rest of the longterm projection period. The alternative fiscal scenario incorporates several changes to current law that are widely expected to occur or that would modify some provisions that might be difficult to sustain for a long period. (For details, see Table 1-1 on page 3.)

CHIP = Children's Health Insurance Program.

Figure A1.Revenues and Primary Spending, by Category, Under CBO's Long-Term Budget Scenarios Through 2080.

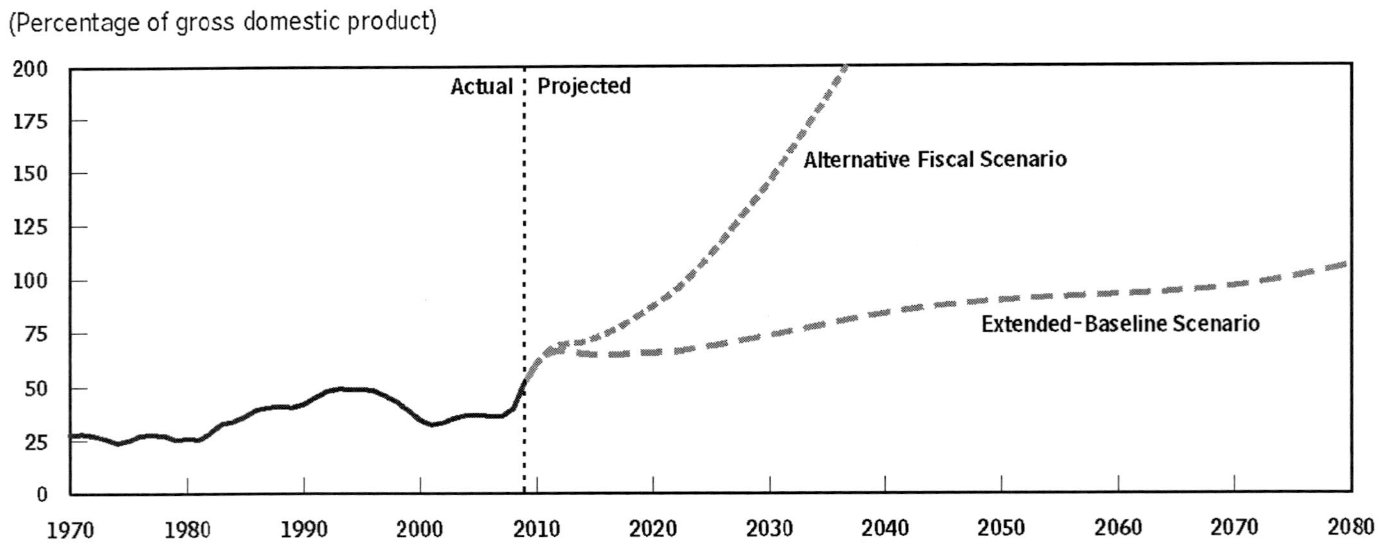

Source: Congressional Budget Office.

Note: The extended-baseline scenario adheres closely to current law, following CBO's 10-year baseline budget projections through 2020 (with adjustments for the recently enacted health care legislation) and then extending the baseline concept for the rest of the longterm projection period. The alternative fiscal scenario incorporates several changes to current law that are widely expected to occur or that would modify some provisions that might be difficult to sustain for a long period. (For details, see Table 1-1 on page 3.)

Figure A2. Federal Debt Held by the Public Under CBO's Long-Term Budget Scenarios Through 2080.

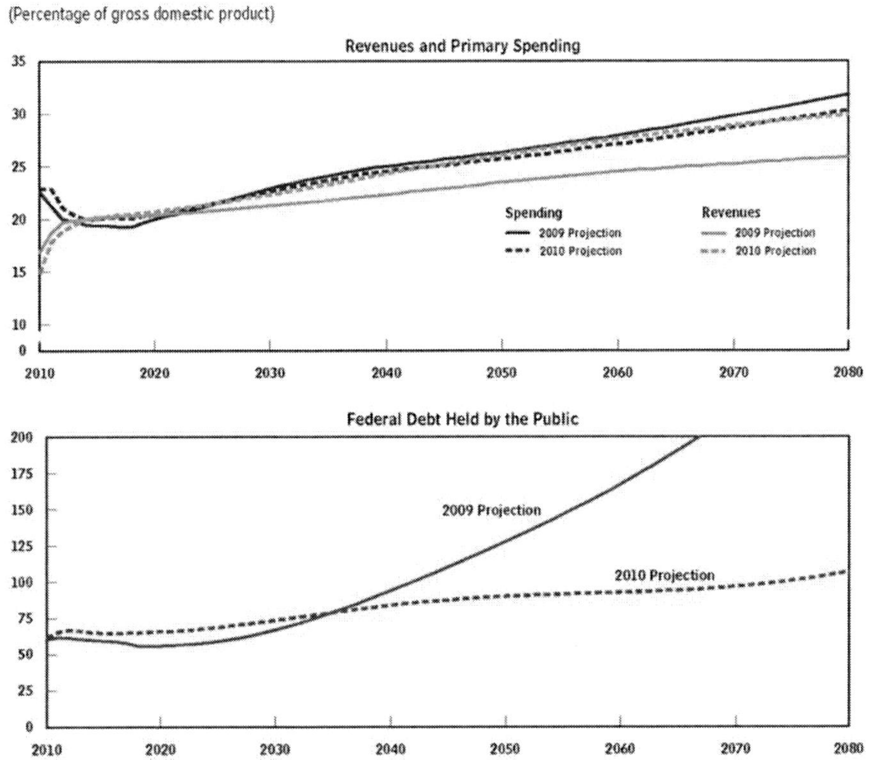

Source: Congressional Budget Office.

Notes: Primary spending refers to all spending other than interest payments on federal debt.

The extended-baseline scenario adheres closely to current law, following CBO's 10-year baseline budget projections through 2020 (with adjustments for the recently enacted health care legislation) and then extending the baseline concept for the rest of the longterm projection period. (For details, see Table 1-1 on page 3.)

Figure A3. Comparison of CBO's 2009 and 2010 Budget Projections Under the Extended-Baseline Scenario Through 2080.

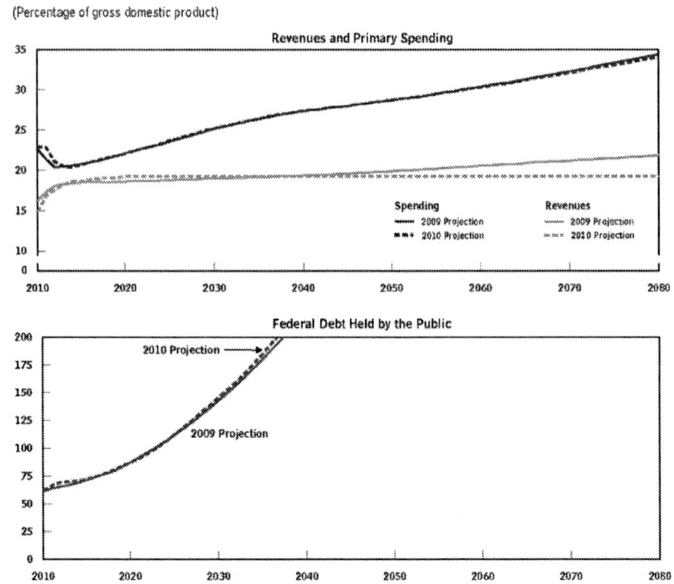

Source: Congressional Budget Office.

Notes: Primary spending refers to all spending other than interest payments on federal debt.

The alternative fiscal scenario incorporates several changes to current law that are widely expected to occur or that would modify some provisions that might be difficult to sustain for a long period. (For details, see Table 1-1 on page 3.)

Figure A4. Comparison of CBO's 2009 and 2010 Budget Projections Under the Alternative Fiscal Scenario Through 2080.

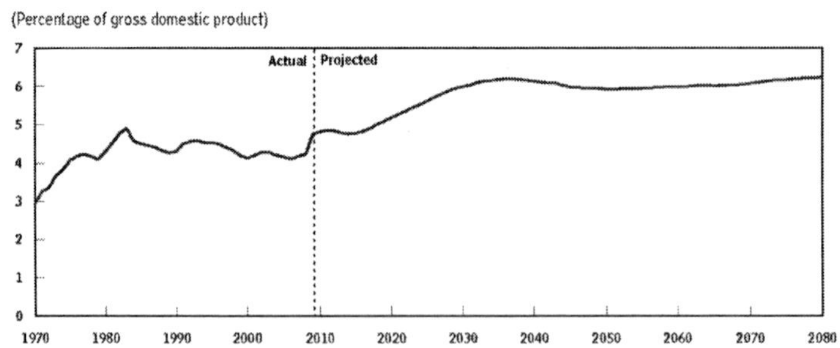

Source: Congressional Budget Office.

Note: Projected spending for Social Security is identical under CBO's two long-term budget scenarios.

Figure A5. Spending for Social Security Under CBO's Long-Term Budget Scenarios Through 2080.

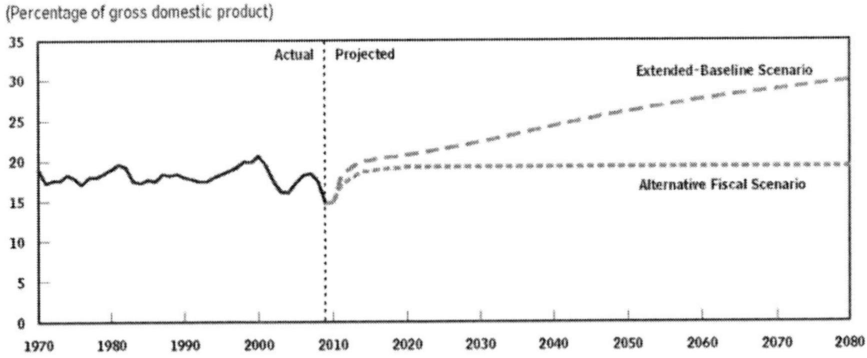

Source: Congressional Budget Office.

Note: The extended-baseline scenario adheres closely to current law, following CBO's 10-year baseline budget projections through 2020 (with adjustments for the recently enacted health care legislation) and then extending the baseline concept for the rest of the longterm projection period. The alternative fiscal scenario incorporates several changes to current law that are widely expected to occur or that would modify some provisions that might be difficult to sustain for a long period. (For details, see Table 1-1 on page 3.)

Figure A6. Total Revenues Under CBO's Long-Term Budget Scenarios Through 2080.

Appendix B. Demographic and Economic Variables Underlying CBO's Analysis

The Congressional Budget Office's (CBO's) longterm budget projections are based on projections for a host of variables that relate to demographic trends and the performance of the U.S. economy. The values for demographic variables used in this analysis come from the most recent annual report of the Social Security trustees.[79] The values for long-term economic variables are based on CBO's 10-year baseline projections as well as on historical economic trends. Those demographic and economic variables are discussed below. (The projections for variables related to the growth in health care costs are discussed in Chapter 2.)

Demographic Variables

Future tax revenues, program spending, and economic performance will all be affected by the size and structure of the U.S. population. For its long-term budget projections, CBO adopted the intermediate (midrange) values in the 2009 report of the Social Security trustees for such demographic variables as the total fertility rate, the rate of decline in mortality, levels of immigration and emigration, and disability rates (specifically, the rates at which people enter and leave Social Security's Disability Insurance program).

Economic Variables

The economic projections in this chapter for 2010 through 2020 are consistent with those in CBO's January 2010 economic forecast, which underlies the agency's current 10-year baseline.[80] For later years, CBO projected stable economic conditions after 2020—in particular, a constant real (inflation-adjusted) interest rate on federal debt and steady growth rates for real wages and gross domestic product (GDP).

CBO projected values for rates of interest, inflation, and unemployment directly. For growth rates of GDP and earnings, in contrast, CBO did not make direct projections but instead derived values for those variables by using other economic and demographic assumptions. (Annual values for selected economic variables through 2084 can be found in the supplementary data for this chapter on CBO's Web site, www.cbo.gov.)

Projections of Interest Rates, Inflation, and Unemployment After 2020

CBO projected that after a 10-year phase-in from the 2020 rate, the real interest rate on 10-year Treasury notes would be 3.0 percent through 2084. Because the average maturity of federal debt is expected to be less than 10 years, CBO projected that the effective interest rate on federal debt held by the public would be slightly lower, averaging 2.7 percent a year. CBO used the same 2.7 percent value as a discount rate for calculating the present value of future streams of total revenues and outlays. The Social Security and Medicare trust funds hold longer- term debt, so the interest rates on those funds were assumed to be 3.0 percent a year. CBO used that value to discount future streams of revenues and outlays for the Social Security and Medicare trust funds.

CBO also projected that annual inflation—as measured by growth in both the consumer price index for urban wage earners and clerical workers (CPI-W) and the consumer price index for all urban consumers (CPI-U)—would be 2.5 percent. The unemployment rate was projected to decline to 5.0 percent and remain at that level over the long run.

Variables Underlying Projections of GDP and Earnings

CBO projected that from 2021 through 2084, real GDP would grow at an average rate of 2.0 percent a year, and real earnings would grow at an average rate of 1.3 percent. Those estimates were based on CBO's demographic assumptions and on four underlying economic projections:

- *Growth in Productivity*—CBO projected that in the long term, total factor productivity (average real output per unit of combined labor and capital services) would grow at an average annual rate of 1.3 percent. CBO incorporated that projection into an economic model that also uses projections of growth in the supply of labor and capital to compute the resulting growth in labor productivity (measured as growth in output per hour worked). The resulting projection for growth in labor productivity averages 1.6 percent a year. That figure differs from the average growth rate for real earnings because labor productivity does not translate directly into earnings growth; the other factors listed below also play a role.
- *Changes in the Ratio of Taxable Earnings to Total Compensation*—The average growth rate of taxable earnings is affected by the share of compensation that workers receive as nontaxable benefits. That share in turn is influenced by the growth of premiums for employment-based health insurance. CBO expects that private-sector costs for health care will grow more quickly than compensation over the long-term projection period (with that difference gradually declining). That trend, by itself, would cause the nontaxable share of compensation to increase over time and the taxable share to decrease. In the near term, however, that effect is likely to be offset by people's responses to the new excise tax on employment-based health insurance plans with relatively high premiums, which is scheduled to take effect in 2018. At least initially, employers who would otherwise be subject to the tax are apt to shift to less expensive health plans to avoid the tax, which will tend to increase the taxable share of compensation. (For more

about the effects of the excise tax, see Chapter 4; for a discussion of trends in costs for health care, see Chapter 2.)

- *Average Hours Worked*—CBO projected that the average number of hours worked by people in each demographic group would remain constant. However, different segments of the population work different numbers of hours, on average. For example, men tend to work more hours than women, and people in their 30s tend to work more hours than people in their 50s. As a result, CBO's projection of total average hours worked declines by 2 percent by 2080 because of projected changes in the composition of the labor force.
- *Difference Between Inflation as Measured by the GDP Deflator and by the CPI*—The GDP deflator and the consumer price index are both used to gauge inflation. The GDP deflator measures the level of prices of all final goods and services produced. The CPI measures the level of consumer prices based on a typical market basket of goods and services. Because of the difference in how the two measures are constructed, there is a gap between the rates at which they grow. CBO projected that the gap would average 0.3 percentage points a year over the long-term projection period. CBO uses the CPI to deflate earnings, because the CPI is a measure of the change in the cost of living for consumers. Thus, the larger the gap between the growth rates of the GDP deflator and the CPI, the more that real earnings growth is reduced.

End Notes

[1] Mandatory programs are ones that do not require annual appropriations by the Congress; the major mandatory health programs consist of Medicare, Medicaid, the Children's Health Insurance Program, and health insurance subsidies that will be provided through the exchanges established by the recently enacted health care legislation.

[2] For details, see Congressional Budget Office, letter to the Honorable Nancy Pelosi about the budgetary effects of H.R. 4872, the Reconciliation Act of 2010 (March 20, 2010), and Chapter 2 of this chapter. If all of its provisions are carried out, the legislation will also increase federal revenues and reduce budget deficits over the 2010–2019 period and in subsequent years, according to estimates by CBO and the staff of the Joint Committee on Taxation.

[3] See Congressional Budget Office, *An Analysis of the President's Budgetary Proposals for Fiscal Year 2011* (March 2010).

[4] CBO's baseline is a benchmark for measuring the budgetary effects of proposed changes to federal revenues or spending. It consists of projections of budget authority, outlays, revenues, and the deficit or surplus over 10 years calculated according to rules set forth in the Balanced Budget and Emergency Deficit Control Act of 1985. Those projections are not

intended to be predictions of future budgetary outcomes; rather, they represent CBO's best judgment of how economic and other factors would affect federal revenues and spending if current laws did not change.

[5] The alternative minimum tax is a parallel income tax system with fewer exemptions, deductions, and rates than the regular income tax. Households must calculate the amount they owe under both the AMT and the regular income tax and pay the larger of the two amounts.

[6] Effective marginal tax rates on labor or capital income represent the percentage of the last dollar of such income that is taken by federal taxes.

[7] Longer-term versions of some of the figures in this chapter are presented in Appendix A.

[8] Mandatory programs are ones that do not require annual appropriations by the Congress; the funding available for them is generally not limited. Most mandatory spending is for entitlement programs, in which the federal government is required to make payments to any person or other entity that meets the eligibility criteria set in law.

[9] Those totals include gross Medicare spending (that is, they do not net out offsetting receipts, which consist mainly of premiums paid by Medicare beneficiaries).

[10] Those projections do not include the effects of recent legislation that delayed the reduction in payment rates until December 2010.

[11] See Congressional Budget Office, letter to the Honorable Nancy Pelosi about the budgetary effects of H.R. 4872, the Reconciliation Act of 2010 (March 20, 2010).

[12] The balances of those trust funds represent the total amount that the government is legally authorized to spend on each program. For a discussion of the legal issues related to trust fund insolvency, see Christine Scott, *Social Security: What Would Happen If the Trust Funds Ran Out?* Report for Congress RL33514 (Congressional Research Service, August 20, 2009).

[13] The total amount of 1.9 percent of GDP includes outlays from the American Recovery and Reinvestment Act of 2009 (Public Law 111-5) and the portion of outlays for unemployment insurance and the Supplemental Nutrition Assistance Program (formerly known as Food Stamps) that CBO estimates would not occur if economic output were at its potential level. For a related discussion, see Congressional Budget Office, *The Effects of Automatic Stabilizers on the Federal Budget* (May 2010).

[14] In Congressional Budget Office, *The Long-Term Budget Outlook* (June 2009), those offsetting receipts were netted against Medicare spending rather than against other spending.

[15] The bulk of payroll tax revenue comes from taxes designated for Social Security and Medicare; smaller amounts come from unemployment insurance taxes and contributions to federal retirement programs.

[16] In contrast, debt held by trust funds and other government accounts—which, together with debt held by the public, make up gross federal debt—represents internal transactions of the government and thus has no effect on credit markets.

[17] The fiscal gap equals the present value of revenues over a given period minus the present value of outlays over that period, adjusted to keep federal debt at its current percentage of GDP. Specifically, current debt is added to the outlay measure, and the present value of the target end-of-period debt (which equals GDP in the last year of the period multiplied by the ratio of debt to GDP at the beginning of 2010) is added to the revenue measure. The present value of a stream of future revenues is computed by taking the revenues for each year, discounting each value to 2010 dollars, and summing the resulting series. The same method is applied to the projected stream of outlays. CBO used a real discount rate equal to the effective interest rate on debt held by the public, which was assumed to be 2.7 percent in the long term.

[18] See Congressional Budget Office, *The Effects of Automatic Stabilizers on the Federal Budget.*

[19] See Congressional Budget Office, *Estimated Impact of the American Recovery and Reinvestment Act on Employment and Economic Output from January 2010 Through March 2010* (May 2010).

[20] Capital inflows can also affect other aspects of the U.S. economy, such as the distribution of income, but those effects are beyond the scope of this analysis.

[21] See Congressional Budget Office, *Long-Term Economic Effects of Chronically Large Federal Deficits*, Issue Brief (October 13, 2005).

[22] The analysis assumed that a percentage-point increase in the rate of return on capital would translate into a percentage-point increase in the interest rate on government debt. That effect is larger than the one CBO assumed in *The Long-Term Budget Outlook* published in June 2009 and is, in CBO's view, more realistic for long-term projections of rising debt. That change in the analysis from 2009 to 2010 increases the projected impact of crowding out.

[23] The difference between the impact of rising debt on GDP and on GNP depends on the rate of return that foreigners receive on capital they invest in the United States. Economic theory suggests that over the long run, there should be little difference between the returns earned by foreigners on their investments in the United States and the returns earned by domestic investors on comparable investments (except for possible differences in taxes paid). However, in recent decades, domestic investors have earned a higher average return on U.S. investments than foreign investors have (adjusted for the apparent riskiness of the investments). For a related discussion, see Congressional Budget Office, *Why Does U.S. Investment Abroad Earn Higher Returns Than Foreign Investment in the United States?* Issue Brief (November 30, 2005). CBO expects that over time, the return earned by foreigners on U.S. investments will move closer to the return earned by domestic investors. That diminishing difference implies that a rising percentage of the GDP generated from additional inflows of foreign capital will be returned to foreign investors as income. For this analysis, that share is assumed to reach 80 percent by 2025 and to remain at that level thereafter.

[24] The economic model used for this comparison is capable of estimating outcomes only under sustainable government policies. Therefore, the analysis had to involve stabilizing the debt-to-GDP ratio at some point rather than allowing it to increase indefinitely. For more details of the analysis, see Congressional Budget Office, *Economic Impacts of Waiting to Resolve the Long-Term Budget Imbalance* (forthcoming).

[25] See Congressional Budget Office, *Federal Debt and the Risk of a Fiscal Crisis*, Issue Brief (July 27, 2010).

[26] See Congressional Budget Office, *The Long-Term Budget Outlook* (June 2009).

[27] In this chapter, federal discretionary spending on health care—that is, spending that is subject to annual appropriations—is included in the budget projections for other noninterest spending (see Table 1-2 in Chapter 1). Some mandatory spending on health care (for example, spending for federal retirees) is also included in other noninterest spending; that mandatory spending represents a very small share of the federal budget.

[28] For further discussion of the challenges of projecting the longterm effects of legislation on federal health care spending, see Congressional Budget Office, letter to the Honorable Max Baucus about different measures for analyzing proposals to reform health care (October 30, 2009).

[29] One factor complicating the comparison is that this year's report presents figures for gross spending for Medicare, whereas last year's report focused on net Medicare spending—that is, gross spending minus certain offsetting receipts (primarily the premiums paid by enrollees). Here, those offsetting receipts (which are projected to total about 1 percent of GDP in 2035) have been excluded from the spending total reported last year for purposes of comparing the two projections.

[30] Some people have coverage from more than one source at a time. Currently, about 7.5 million people with Medicaid coverage are also covered by Medicare, which is their primary source of coverage. All of the estimates reflect average monthly enrollments during the year.

[31] This chapter defines "total health care spending" as spending for health care services and supplies as defined in the national health expenditure accounts maintained by the Centers for Medicare and Medicaid Services. That concept excludes spending on medical research,

structures, and equipment. Under a broader definition that includes those categories, total national health expenditures in 2008 were 16.2 percent of GDP.

[32] In this analysis, out-of-pocket payments do not include the premiums that people pay for health insurance (because premiums fund the payments that insurers provide, which are already included in the measure of private spending).

[33] Various other sources, including a portion of the federal income taxes that people pay on their Social Security benefits, provide the remainder of the funding for Medicare.

[34] Estimates are based on information in Medicare Payment Advisory Commission, *A Data Book: Healthcare Spending and the Medicare Program* (June 2009), p. 61.

[35] See Kaiser Commission on Medicaid and the Uninsured, *Medicaid Enrollment and Spending by "Mandatory" and "Optional" Eligibility and Benefit Categories* (Washington, D.C.:

[36] Under certain conditions, parents of enrolled children are also eligible for CHIP, but they constitute a very small percentage of the program's enrollment.

[37] See Congressional Budget Office, *Technological Change and the Growth of Health Care Spending* (January 2008).

[38] For additional discussion, see Congressional Budget Office, *Key Issues in Analyzing Major Health Insurance Proposals* (December 2008), p. 23.

[39] Sheila Smith, Joseph P. Newhouse, and Mark S. Freeland, "Income, Insurance, and Technology: Why Does Health Spending Outpace Economic Growth?" *Health Affairs*, vol. 28, no. 5 (September/October 2009), pp. 1276–1284.

[40] Amy Finkelstein, "The Aggregate Effects of Health Insurance: Evidence from the Introduction of Medicare," *Quarterly Journal of Economics*, vol. 122, no. 1 (February 2007), pp. 1–37. One factor that may have contributed to that study's findings was the relatively generous payment system that Medicare adopted. Following the common practice of private insurers at the time, Medicare initially paid hospitals on the basis of their incurred costs—an approach that gave hospitals little incentive to control those costs. The increase in hospital spending that resulted from Medicare's creation might have been smaller under a less generous payment system.

[41] For Medicare, CBO also adjusts for changes in the projected life expectancy (time until death) of beneficiaries. For Medicaid, CBO adjusts for changes in the program's case mix—that is, the portions of beneficiaries who are children, disabled people, elderly people, and other adults—rather than for changes in age composition. The introduction of Medicare's Part D drug benefit in 2006 resulted in a one-time shift in some spending from Medicaid to Medicare; to adjust for that shift, CBO assumed that excess cost growth in 2006 for both Medicare and Medicaid was equal to the average of excess cost growth in the two programs for that year.

[42] After 2020, spending on CHIP was held constant as a share of GDP.

[43] In last year's report, the rates of excess cost growth in the final year of the 75-year projection period were 0.1 percentage point for Medicaid and all other health care spending and 0.9 percentage points for Medicare.

[44] PPACA expanded eligibility for Medicaid to include nonelderly residents with income up to 133 percent of the federal poverty level. A provision of the Health Care and Education Reconciliation Act of 2010 effectively increased that threshold to 138 percent of the FPL. The FPL is currently $22,050 for a family of four.

[45] To the extent that receiving a tax credit reduces what a person owes in taxes, the credit results in a reduction in revenues. Because the tax credits are refundable, however, people can receive a credit that exceeds their income tax liability, in which case a cash payment will be made for the portion beyond the liability; such payments appear in the federal budget as outlays.

[46] For a further description of accountable care organizations, see Congressional Budget Office, *Budget Options Volume I: Health Care* (December 2008), pp. 72–74.

[47] The additional indexing factor will apply in any year (after 2018) in which the total costs of exchange subsidies exceed a specified percentage of GDP; CBO expects that condition will probably be met.

[48] See Congressional Budget Office, letter to the Honorable Nancy Pelosi about the budgetary effects of H.R. 4872.

[49] CBO also estimated the effects of the legislation on the "federal budgetary commitment to health care," a term that describes the sum of net federal outlays for health programs and tax preferences for health care (such as the tax exclusion for employment-based health insurance). Specifically, CBO estimated that the two laws will increase that commitment by about $390 billion over the 2010–2019 period. In subsequent years, however, the effects of the provisions of the laws that will tend to decrease the federal budgetary commitment to health care will exceed the effects of the provisions that will increase it. As a result, CBO expects that, relative to prior law, the legislation will generate a net reduction in the federal budgetary commitment to health care during the 2020–2029 period. For additional discussion of that term, see Congressional Budget Office, letter to the Honorable Max Baucus about different measures for analyzing current proposals to reform health care. In this chapter, the effects of the legislation on tax preferences for health care and tax revenues more generally are examined in Chapter 4.

[50] For the alternative fiscal scenario, CBO assumed that Medicare's payment rates for physicians would be held constant in 2010 at the 2009 amounts and then increased annually through 2020 using the Medicare economic index—a measure of input costs for physicians' services, adjusted for productivity gains. After 2020, Medicare's spending on physicians' services is combined with all other Medicare spending, which is projected to grow using the assumptions described above.

[51] CBO assumed that under both scenarios, Medicare benefits would continue to be paid in full regardless of the financial status of the Hospital Insurance Trust Fund.

[52] For an analysis of the relative impacts that aging of the population and excess cost growth have on the projections, see Box 1-2 in Chapter 1.

[53] The estimates from last year's report have been adjusted to reflect gross spending for Medicare, rather than net spending, to make them comparable with the estimates in this year's report.

[54] In last year's report, the projections for Medicaid did not include spending for CHIP; however, spending on that program is relatively small (about $7 billion in 2008), representing less than one- tenth of 1 percent of GDP.

[55] A present value is a single number that expresses a flow of current and future income or payments in terms of an equivalent lump sum received or paid today. Here, it is calculated over 75 years using a 3 percent real discount rate.

[56] The imbalances that CBO projected last year were also larger than those projected by the Medicare program's trustees. In 2009, the trustees projected an actuarial imbalance equal to 3.9 percent of taxable payroll over 75 years. One reason for the difference from CBO's previous projection is that the trustees assumed a lower rate of excess cost growth in Medicare—averaging about 1 percentage point per year over the projection period. The trustees have not yet released their 2010 estimate of the actuarial imbalance.

[57] See Congressional Budget Office, letter to the Honorable Jeff Sessions providing additional information on the effect of the Patient Protection and Affordable Care Act on the Hospital Insurance Trust Fund (January 22, 2010).

[58] See Congressional Budget Office, *Social Security Disability Insurance: Participation Trends and Their Fiscal Implications*, Issue Brief (forthcoming).

[59] CBO projects that the continuing rapid growth of health care costs will reduce the portion of compensation that workers receive in wages subject to the Social Security payroll tax. That reduction will lower the growth of both Social Security revenues and benefits relative to what would occur if health care costs grew more slowly.

[60] The outlook for the baby boomers' financial situation in retirement is summarized in Congressional Budget Office, *The Retirement Prospects of the Baby Boomers*, Issue Brief (March 18, 2004); for details, see Congressional Budget Office, *Baby Boomers' Retirement Prospects: An Overview* (November 2003). See also Congressional Budget Office, *Will the Demand for Assets Fall When the Baby Boomers Retire?*, Background Paper (September 2009).

[61] For details on CBO's methodology for projecting Social Security's revenues and outlays, see *CBO's Long-Term Projections for Social Security: 2009 Update* (August 2009).

[62] Those projections do not incorporate the economic effects of the two scenarios.

[63] For information about CBO's projections of total income taxes under the two scenarios, see Chapter 4. For details on the impact of differing assumptions about income taxes on Social Security benefits, see Congressional Budget Office, *The Outlook for Social Security* (June 2004), Box 3-1, pp. 24–25.

[64] To account for the difference between the trust fund's current balance and the desired balance at the end of the period, the balance at the beginning of the time frame is added to the projected revenues and an additional year of costs at the end of the period is added to projected outlays. The present value is a single number that expresses a flow of current and future income or payments in terms of an equivalent lump sum received or paid today.

[65] CBO anticipates that the Disability Insurance trust fund will be exhausted in 2018 (under both scenarios) and that the Old-Age and Survivors Insurance trust fund will be exhausted in 2042 under the extended-baseline scenario and 2040 under the alternative fiscal scenario. However, this study focuses on the combined trust funds. In 1994, the Social Security Trustees' Report projected that the DI trust fund would be exhausted in 1995. That outcome was prevented by legislation that redirected revenue from the OASI trust fund to the DI trust fund. In part because of that experience, it is a common analytical convention to consider the DI and OASI trust funds as combined.

[66] See section 257 of the Balanced Budget and Emergency Deficit Control Act of 1985, P.L. 99-177, as amended; 2 U.S.C. 907.

[67] See Congressional Budget Office, *Social Security Policy Options* (forthcoming).

[68] In recent years, the Congress has enacted temporary increases in the AMT exemption amounts, but the last increase expired at the end of 2009.

[69] The long-term revenue projections reflect the assumption that economic conditions are stable after 2020 and thus exclude the effects of rising taxes on people's behavior.

[70] The parameters of the tax system are the amounts that define the various tax brackets, the personal exemption and standard deduction amounts, and tax rates.

[71] Technically, a taxpayer owes the regular income tax plus any amount that, under the AMT, exceeds the regular tax. For more information on the AMT, see Congressional Budget Office,

[72] *The Individual Alternative Minimum Tax*, Issue Brief (January 15, 2010).

[73] Contributions to some 401(k) plans and individual retirement accounts are not tax-deductible, but withdrawals from those accounts are untaxed.

[74] The thresholds are initially set in statute for 2018 and are indexed to general inflation plus 1 percent for 2019 and to general inflation for 2020 and subsequent years.

[75] While the incremental effect of the excise tax is uncertain, the excise tax reduces uncertainty in the overall revenue forecast by limiting the impact of untaxed health insurance benefits. Prior to the introduction of the excise tax, the size of the untaxed benefits depended upon the future path of health care spending. By limiting the impact of the untaxed health benefits on the revenue base, the excise tax reduces that source of uncertainty.

[76] See Congressional Budget Office, letter to the Honorable Nancy Pelosi about the budgetary effects of H.R. 4872, the Reconciliation Act of 2010 (March 20, 2010).

[77] Although the Statutory Pay-As-You-Go Act of 2010 provides only for the temporary extension of the 2009 estate tax parameters and alternative minimum tax relief through 2011, the alternative fiscal scenario assumes that both of those policies would continue through 2020.

[78] The additional tax on earnings applies to a greater share of labor income over time because the $250,000 threshold will not be indexed for inflation. The excise tax on certain high-premium plans affects a larger share of compensation over time because the threshold for the tax rises with general prices, while health costs are rising at a faster rate.

[79] The examples assume all income received by taxpayers is compensation. For details about the calculations, see Table 4-4.

[80] Social Security Administration, *The 2009 Annual Report of the Board of Trustees of the Federal Old-Age and Survivors Insurance and Federal Disability Insurance Trust Funds* (May 12, 2009). The trustees have not yet released their 2010 report.

[81] See Congressional Budget Office, *The Budget and Economic Outlook: Fiscal Years 2010 to 2020* (January 2010), Chapter 2.

In: The Long-Term Budget Outlook
Editor: Jessica C. Anderson

ISBN: 978-1-61122-190-9

Chapter 2

THE ECONOMIC IMPLICATIONS OF THE LONG-TERM FEDERAL BUDGET OUTLOOK

Marc Labonte

SUMMARY

Following the financial crisis, the budget deficit reached 10% of GDP in 2009, a level that cannot be sustained in the long run. Concerns about long-term fiscal sustainability depend on the projected future path of the budget, absent future policy changes. The retirement of the baby boomers, rising life expectancy, and the rising cost of medical care result in projections of large and growing budget deficits over the next several decades. Social Security outlays are projected to rise from 4.8% of gross domestic product (GDP) today to 6.0% of GDP in 2035, and Medicare and Medicaid outlays are projected to rise from 5.3% today to as much as 10.0% of GDP in 2035 and 12.7% of GDP in 2050. These increases in spending are not expected to subside after the baby boomers have passed away. Without any corresponding rise in revenues, this spending path would lead to unsustainably large and persistent budget deficits, which would push up interest rates and the trade deficit, crowd out private investment spending, and ultimately cause fiscal crisis.

To avoid this outcome, taxes would need to be raised or expenditures would need to be reduced. Altering taxes and benefits ahead of time would reduce the size of adjustments required in the future, if the proceeds were used to increase national saving. (Making changes ahead of time would also allow individuals time to adjust their private saving behavior.) National saving can be increased by using the proceeds to pay down the national debt, purchase financial securities, or finance individual accounts. But if the budget savings is offset by new spending or tax cuts, the government's ability to finance future benefits will not have improved. Individual accounts financed by increasing the budget deficit, however, would not increase national saving or reduce the government's fiscal imbalance and could exacerbate the government's fiscal imbalance over the 75-year projection.

Relatively small tax increases or benefit reductions could return Social Security to long-run solvency. Restraining the growth in Medicare and Medicaid spending is more uncertain and difficult, however. The projected increase in spending is driven more by medical spending outpacing general spending increases than by demographic change. But it is uncertain how to restrain cost growth because much of it is the result of technological innovation that makes new and expensive treatments available. If future medical spending grows more slowly than projected, then the long-term budget outlook improves dramatically. From a government-wide perspective, Social Security or Medicare trust fund assets cannot help finance future benefits because they are redeemed with general revenues at a time when the overall budget is in deficit.

The reason revenues are not projected to rise along with outlays is that these programs are financed on a pay-as-you-go basis: current workers finance the benefits of current retirees. In the future, there will be fewer workers per retiree. Once a pay-as-you-go system is up and running and faced with an adverse demographic shift, there is no reform that can avoid making some present or future generation receive less than past generations. Under current policy, future generations will be made worse off by higher taxes or lower benefits. Under a reform that increases national saving, some of that burden would be shifted to current generations. Overall, current budget deficits negate the system's limited existing prefunding, exacerbating the future fiscal shortfall. While entitlement spending on the elderly is the major driver behind future deficits, it played little part in the growth of the current budget deficit. Reducing the current deficit is the most straightforward and concrete step that can be taken today to reduce the future shortfall.

The United States is projected to undergo a demographic shift as the aging of the baby boomers causes an unprecedented increase in the fraction of the population that is retired. Coupled with rising life expectancy, this means, under current policy, a steady increase in the portion of the population that is both out of the workforce and receiving social insurance benefits from the government. At the same time, the cost of health care has persistently outpaced income growth, and may continue to do so while an aging population is utilizing more health care. If left unattended, this situation poses serious challenges for the government's fiscal position and the economy as a whole.[1]

Following the financial crisis, the budget deficit reached 10% of GDP in 2009, a level that cannot be sustained in the long run. Concerns about long-term fiscal sustainability depend on the projected future path of the budget, absent future policy changes. While the recent growth in the budget deficit was due to short-term developments unrelated to entitlement spending on the elderly, the projected path of the budget in the long run primarily depends on the future path of entitlement spending.[2] This chapter analyzes the long-run path of the federal budget; for a discussion of the current fiscal situation, see CRS Report R40770, *Economic Effects of a Budget Deficit Exceeding $1 Trillion.*

PROJECTIONS SHOW THAT CURRENT FISCAL POLICY IS UNSUSTAINABLE

Social Security and Medicare are financed primarily on a pay-as-you-go basis: benefits paid to today's elderly are based on dedicated payroll taxes collected from today's workers.[3] Under current policy, expenditures are projected to grow much more rapidly than revenues because of the increase in retirees relative to workers. The worker to recipient ratio for Social Security is shown in Figure 1 and is projected to fall from 3.2 workers per recipient in 2008 to 2.2 workers per recipient in 2030. (The worker to recipient ratio for Medicare is slightly lower than for Social Security, but exhibits the same pattern over the long-run projection.) The projected decline in the worker to recipient ratio is driven by the retirement of the baby boomers, declining fertility, and increasing life expectancy, which means that, under current policy and retirement patterns, workers will be spending a larger fraction of their lives in retirement (assuming workers' and employers' attitudes toward retirement do not change). Thus, the increases in spending are not projected to subside after the baby boomers have passed away. Worker to recipient forecasts are subject to large margins of uncertainty, represented by the high and low lines in the graph. But even under the most optimistic of assumptions about population growth, the worker to recipient ratio will fall well below historical levels in coming years.

For elderly entitlement spending to keep in line with revenues in light of these demographic changes, some combination of expenditures reduction and revenue increase will be required. Social Security and Medicare are financed through dedicated revenues: the payroll (FICA) tax. As shown below, diverting existing general revenues to entitlement spending cannot realistically cover the financing gap because of the sheer magnitude of the gap relative to total government revenues. Thus, the financing problem should not be thought of as a programmatic problem, but rather as a government-wide problem, and is best analyzed relative to economic output (GDP). (The role of the Social Security and Medicare trust funds will be discussed below.)

Figure 2 illustrates the projected increase in Social Security spending from the present to 2105. Projected spending increases from 4.8% of GDP in 2008 to 5.8% of GDP in 2058, whereas revenues are projected to stay fairly constant as a proportion of GDP. However, there is a high degree of uncertainty surrounding these projections. The Congressional Budget Office (CBO) estimates that there is a 10% chance that spending will exceed 7.0% of GDP by 2058, and a 10% chance that spending will be below 4.9% of GDP that year. By contrast, revenue projections show a very narrow degree of uncertainty as a share of GDP, so that under almost any scenario a large shortfall between revenues and spending is projected.[4]

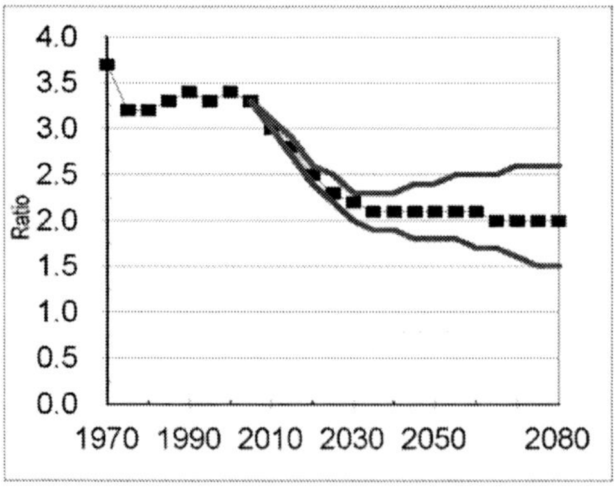

Source. Trustees of OASDI, Annual Report, 2009, Table IV.B2.

Note. Middle line based on Trustees' intermediate assumptions. Outside lines represent worker-recipient ratios under alternative scenarios. Beneficiaries include the retired, survivors, dependents, and the disabled.

Figure 1. Worker to Recipient Ratio for Social Security, 1970-2080.

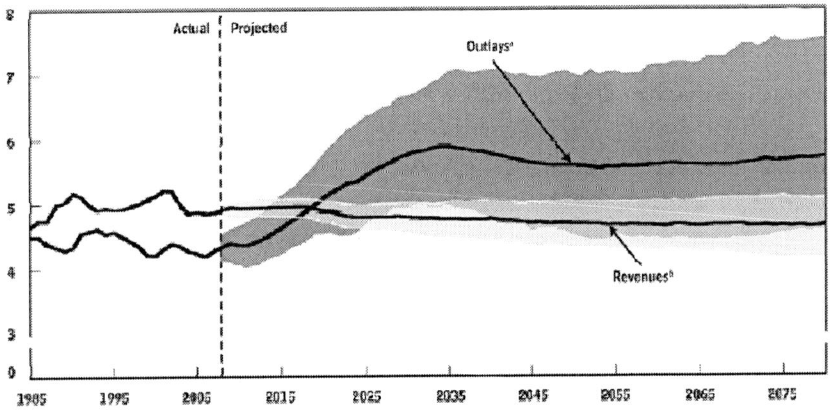

Source: Congressional Budget Office, Updated Long-Term Projections for Social Security, August 2008.

Notes: The dark lines indicate CBO's projections of expected outcomes. Shaded areas indicate the 80 percent range of uncertainty around each projection based on a distribution of 500 simulations from CBO's long-term model. (An 80 percent range means that there is a 10 percent chance that actual values will be above that range, a 10 percent chance that they will be below it, and an 80 percent chance that they will fall within the range.) In the scheduled benefits scenario, workers each year receive full benefits as calculated under current law.

[a] Includes scheduled benefits and administrative costs.

[b] Includes payroll taxes and revenues from the taxation of benefits.

Figure 2. Social Security Spending and Revenues as a % of GDP.

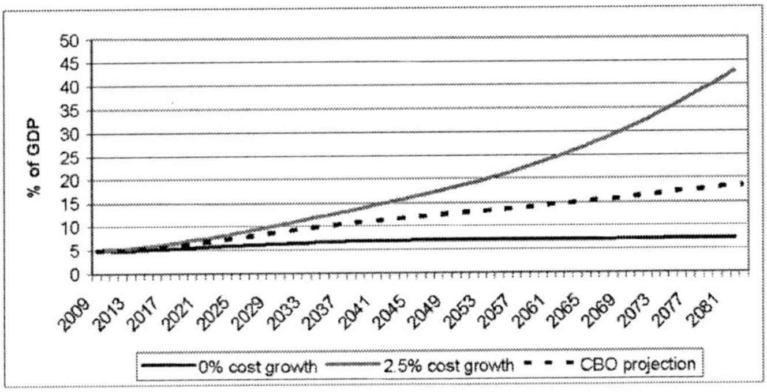

Source. Congressional Budget Office, *The Long-Term Budget Outlook*, June 2009.

Note. Excess cost growth refers to growth in spending per beneficiary above GDP per capita growth.

Figure 3. Projected Spending for Medicare and Medicaid as a % of GDP Under Various Assumptions about Excess Cost Growth.

Social Security projections are based on straightforward assumptions since benefits are determined by specific rules and formulas and demographic projections. By contrast, there is no obvious way to project Medicare and Medicaid spending into the future because widely differing assumptions can be made about how much will be spent per beneficiary under current law.[5] While there are fairly reliable projections of the number of Medicare beneficiaries, and current law broadly specifies the medical services that Medicare and Medicaid will cover, little can be known about how medical treatments, costs, and technologies will evolve in the future, or what new treatments will become available in the future. New technologies could potentially lower costs through productivity gains, but they could also potentially raise costs by making new treatments available that are both more effective and more expensive.

In recent history, the latter has occurred, and as a result health spending has risen more rapidly than GDP (referred to as *excess cost growth*). However, there is no guarantee that this pattern will continue in the future. In fact, it is unreasonable to extrapolate historical excess cost growth indefinitely, since that would result in health care eventually consuming 100% of GDP.[6] Unfortunately, although there is great uncertainty about what future rate of excess cost growth above growth in GDP per capita is reasonable, Medicare and Medicaid expenditure projections are highly sensitive to this assumption. To illustrate the sensitivity, Figure 3 compares CBO's projection of Medicare and Medicaid spending to two other scenarios: that the historical growth rates of 2.5% persisted and that excess cost growth is eliminated.[7]

CBO's projection is based on the assumption that excess cost growth will eventually slow down enough to allow non-health consumption to grow modestly (in absolute terms). Specifically, CBO assumes that excess cost growth will slow from 2.3% in 2020 to 0.9% in 2083 for Medicare and from 1.9% in 2020 to 0.1% in 2083 for Medicaid. (Medicaid cost growth slows more because, although CBO cannot assume that current federal policy can change, it can assume that state policy would change, and Medicaid is a jointly financed federal-state program.) In CBO's projection, combined Medicare and Medicaid spending increase from 5.3% in 2009 to as much as 10.0% in 2035 and 12.7% of GDP in 2050, at which point total health care spending is projected to exceed one-third of GDP. Medicare's dedicated revenues are also projected to stay relatively constant, so even under the most benign scenarios, these programs would put a serious strain on general revenues under current policy.[8] Even with the assumption that excess cost growth will slow, total health care spending (private and public) would be nearly half of GDP by the end of the projection window.

Although most of the policy debate in the past has focused on ways to reform Social Security, it is Medicare and Medicaid that place a far larger strain on the federal budget. Between now and 2035, Social Security spending is projected to increase by 1.2 percentage points, whereas Medicare and Medicaid spending is projected to increase by as much as 4.7 percentage points of GDP. From 2035 to 2050, Social Security spending as a share of GDP is projected to decrease by 0.3 percentage points, whereas Medicare and Medicaid spending is projected to increase by 2.7 percentage points.

Other government spending programs will also be affected by an aging society, including Supplemental Security Income (SSI) and health and pension spending for civil servants and veterans.[9] Some analysts fear that the finances of the Pension Benefit Guarantee Corporation, a government agency that insures private defined benefit pension plans, could also be negatively affected if firms do not take steps to improve their pension reserves.[10] (On the other hand, government spending on the young could fall as a share of GDP as our society ages, although much of that spending is done at the state level.) The increase in projected spending for these programs is small as a share of GDP compared with the increases in Social Security, Medicaid, and Medicare spending, however. In 2000, Social Security, Medicare, and Medicaid accounted for about 85% of total federal spending on the elderly.[11]

It is also unclear what assumptions should be made to project current tax policy. If current law were followed, the 2001 and 2003 tax cuts would expire and an estimated 70% of taxpayers would eventually be subject to the alternative minimum tax (AMT) due to inflation. A projection more consistent with current tax policy would arguably be to assume that the tax cuts do not expire and the AMT is indexed for inflation. This projection results in a modest increase in revenues relative to GDP because of "real bracket creep," meaning that as incomes rise, taxpayers on average shift into higher tax brackets.[12] Likewise, discretionary spending is set annually through the appropriations process, so many valid assumptions could be made about its future size. An assumption that nondefense discretionary spending will stay close to its recent share of GDP is consistent with recent history and seems reasonable for a long-term projection.

Under the above assumptions about current policy and future excess cost growth, the increase in entitlement spending would not be matched by increases in general revenues or decreases in other spending, and would need to be entirely deficit financed. As a result, after briefly dipping to 7.4% of

GDP in 2020, projected budget deficits would top 14% of GDP by 2035 and the national debt would rise at a continually accelerating pace and rapidly surpass record levels relative to GDP. If the tax cuts and AMT patch were assumed to expire (as scheduled under current law) and non- entitlement spending were reduced to all-time lows relative to GDP, deficits would rise more slowly, but still exceed 10% of GDP after 2050.

Another way to measure the imbalance in future government finances is through the fiscal gap concept, which refers to the immediate reduction in spending or increase in taxes that would be required in order to prevent the federal debt from rising relative to GDP over the projection window.[13] CBO estimates a fiscal gap of 8.1% of GDP over the next 75 years under current policy. To close this fiscal gap today, would require immediately reducing total non-interest spending by 32%, raising total revenues by 52%, or some combination of the two. Although these changes would be unprecedented, delay would require even larger cuts in the future. Waiting until 2020 to change policy would increase the fiscal gap to 9.7% of GDP, and waiting until 2040 would increase it to 15.5% of GDP, necessitating more drastic adjustments. Although these options are undesirable, they cannot be postponed indefinitely (if the projections prove to be accurate) for reasons discussed in the next section. Policymakers do have a wide array of choices concerning the form the tax increases or spending cuts could take, however.

The Effects of Current Policy on the Economy

Figure 4 illustrates why current policy is considered to be unsustainable. Large budget deficits would cause the national debt to rise at an accelerating rate to unprecedented levels. If current policy is maintained, the deficit would decline to 7.4% in 2020, which would not be small enough to prevent the debt from continuing to grow relative to GDP. After 2020, the deficit would rise rapidly.

Before 2009, the United States had never financed a peacetime deficit above 6% of GDP and foreign countries have not succeeded in financing persistent deficits that were much larger. Although larger U.S. deficits were financed during wars, wars are only temporary, whereas the fiscal imbalance under current law is permanent. In essence, the rise in entitlement spending under a scenario with continued excess cost growth is too large and permanent to credibly be financed indefinitely by pushing its cost forward through borrowing.

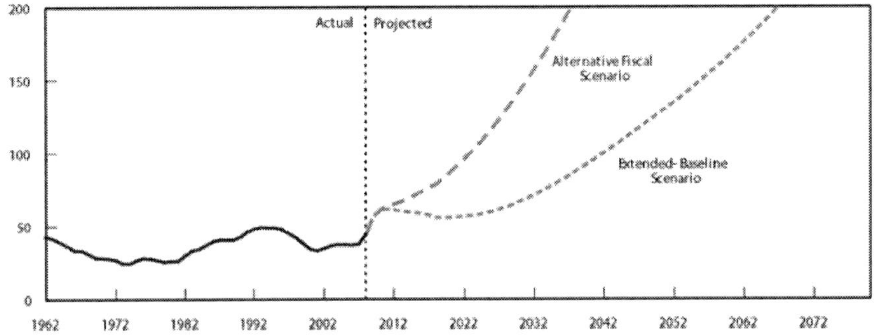

Source: Congressional Budget Office, *The Long-Term Budget Outlook*, June 2009.

Notes: The alternative fiscal scenario assumes that current policy is maintained. The extended-baseline scenario assumes that the tax cuts and AMT patch expire and discretionary spending grows at the rate of inflation for the next 10 years.

Figure 4. Projected Federal Debt as a Share of GDP.

If current policy is maintained and the assumptions in the projections hold, the resulting deficits would likely cause interest rates on U.S. Treasury bonds to rise substantially, both as a result of the higher risk that the Treasury might ultimately default on its debt and also because the government's demand for borrowed funds would raise the price of credit, which is the rate of interest. Default would likely undermine financial stability because of the central role that U.S. Treasury securities play in providing the financial system with liquidity, as a benchmark asset, and as a "safe haven" for risk averse investors. If the government financed its rising budget deficit by increasing the money supply, the rate of inflation would also increase significantly along with interest rates. Budget deficits of the size projected under current law could lead investors to doubt that the United States would be able to service its debt fully and on time, which could cause the value of the dollar to drop precipitously. Because more than one-half of the total outstanding debt of the United States is held abroad, a collapse of the dollar would have serious economic repercussions around the world.

Presumably, U.S. budget policies will be altered before this point is reached. In the interim, the deficit would still have a negative impact on the economy long before the fiscal outlook reached crisis. A rising risk premium due to an unsustainable fiscal policy is only one reason for interest rates to rise. The deficit also causes interest rates to rise because it is competing with private capital investment to be financed from a finite pool of loanable funds from domestic and foreign lenders. Interest rates rise to equilibrate the higher demand for credit with the supply of loanable funds, which is national saving plus capital from abroad. The deficits projected under current policy would exceed private saving and cause national saving to become negative.

Whatever the cause of the increase in interest rates, the effect on the economy is the same: higher interest rates reduce private capital investment. Lower rates of capital formation cause economic growth to slow, leading to lower U.S. living standards (as measured by per capita income) in the long run than there otherwise would have been. Foreign capital flows can offset part or all of the decline in national saving, but this will still result in lower U.S. standards of living than if the budget had been balanced because the income from that capital will flow to foreigners instead of Americans.[14] CBO estimates that, by 2045, the deficits resulting from current policy would reduce the capital stock by more than 35% and gross national product by 16% relative to what it would have been.

Even if future budget deficits were reduced to the point where they became sustainable, crowding out still results in a smaller future economy than would otherwise be the case, all else equal. As a result, fewer resources would be available in the future from which the government can draw to finance the retirement of the baby boomers. Ultimately, the resources available in the economy as a whole will determine the level of government spending that is feasible in the future. Financing a given level of spending from an economy that is smaller than it would have been in the absence of deficits would, in turn, require higher tax rates.

CBO long-term budget projections do not include any of the macroeconomic effects discussed in this section—the projected deficits are not assumed to affect interest rates or GDP through crowding out effects. If macroeconomic effects were included, the projections would be more unfavorable—interest payments on the national debt would be higher and tax revenues would be lower.

Why Can't the Contributions of Young Workers Finance the Benefits that they Have Been Promised?

Proposals to eliminate the shortfall of revenues in the future to finance the entitlement benefits that have been promised under current law have raised criticisms about fairness. After all, retirees today paid the same or lower tax rates than today's workers, and they are receiving the benefits equal to (or exceeding) what they were promised. While this predicament may be perceived as unfair, it is inherent in a pay-as-you-go system where benefits are based on income and financed by those working at the time. When the worker-retiree ratio falls, only two options are available under pay-as-you-go: benefits to retirees fall or taxes on workers rise. A pay-as-you-go system is fundamentally different from the fully funded pension systems that private employers run, where an employee's contributions are invested to finance his future benefits, rather than used to pay the benefits of current retirees. (Even a fully funded pension system would pay smaller monthly annuities when life expectancy rose, however.)

Once a pay-as-you-go system is up and running and suffers an adverse demographic shift, there is no reform that can avoid placing a burden on some participants in the system by making some present or future generation receive less than past generations. This burden can be thought of in terms of generations participating in the system, rather than in terms of taxes and benefits. For example, the burden imposed by a tax on today's workers is equivalent to the burden of a benefit cut when today's workers retire. Reform cannot avoid making some current or future generations pay disproportionately because the windfalls initially created by a pay-as-you-go system have already been collected and spent by the early workers in the system who received benefits that far exceeded their contributions.[15]

Evaluating the generational equity of a reform proposal is best done from a government-wide perspective, and not from a programmatic perspective. For example, proposals can appear to raise entitlement benefits paid to any given generation through general revenue transfers or increasing the national debt. But general revenue transfers or a larger national debt must (eventually) be financed through higher taxes or lower government spending. Thus, the burden has been shifted out of the program and into the general budget—it has not been reduced.

Trust Funds Cannot Finance Future Benefits From A Government- Wide Perspective

According to law, when benefit costs of Social Security and Medicare Part A exceed income, their trust funds can be drawn down to finance benefits. It is often argued that benefits can be financed in full until their trust funds are exhausted, which is projected to occur in 2036 and 2016, respectively. (Medicare Part B does not have a dedicated revenue source and relies heavily on general revenue transfers already.)[16] While this is true from the programs' perspective, the trust fund "assets" have no effect on solvency from the overall government's perspective. The trust funds hold U.S. Treasury securities, which are nothing more than an IOU from the government to the trust fund. Therefore, Social Security and Medicare can only be financed in full as long as the government can find the budgetary resources to finance them. Arguing that the trust fund securities provide those resources is equivalent to arguing that one has assets because one's right pocket contains an IOU from one's left pocket. The problem is not that, from the trust fund's perspective, the government will not honor its Treasury securities. The problem is that, from the government's perspective, it must find the budgetary resources to honor those securities. Under current policy, it will lack the resources before the trust funds are exhausted because tax revenue is not projected to rise nor nonentitlement spending projected to fall in tandem with the rise in entitlement spending.

If the trust fund surpluses created future budgetary resources at the time they were accumulated, then those surpluses could be thought of as having a valid economic "claim" on those resources (although the political process would still determine whether they received their claim). Unfortunately, the government's overall fiscal position has precluded the possible use of the surpluses to create future budgetary resources. With the exception of 1999-2000, surpluses of the Social Security and Medicare systems have not been—and are still not being—used to improve the government's fiscal condition in preparation for the retirement of the baby boomers. Instead, they are being used to support the government's current fiscal stance, in which revenues and other outlays are set at a level where they are not in balance. If the surpluses were being saved, they could be given "credit" for freeing up future budgetary resources, and an argument could be made that those freed-up resources should then be devoted to the entitlement programs. But since they are being diverted to finance nonentitlement spending, the presence of trust fund surpluses has not created any future budgetary resources that can be used by future governments to honor the Treasury securities held by the trust funds. It is the government's unwillingness to balance revenues and outlays outside the trust funds that prevents the trust fund surpluses from generating real resources that can be drawn down in the future.[17]

Focusing the reform debate on the government's overall fiscal position rather than the position of the program's trust fund also would have the benefit of avoiding budgetary maneuvers that may give the false appearance that the programs' fiscal position has been improved. For example, some reform proposals return the trust funds to solvency through general revenue transfers or by "investing" the entitlement surpluses in nongovernmental financial assets (either collectively or through individual accounts) without increasing the government's tax revenue. Although these proposals make the programs' financial position look improved in isolation, they do nothing to reduce the overall imbalance between government outlays and government revenues. In the case of the latter, surpluses diverted from financing general government outlays for "investment" purposes must be replaced by increasing the national debt in the absence of other policy changes. For the government as a whole, higher earnings on the trust funds or individual accounts are offset by higher interest on the national debt.

ECONOMIC EFFECTS OF REFORM OPTIONS

Reform may encompass several goals—altering the redistributive characteristics of the system, giving people more choices about the form their benefits take, and so on. This section considers reform options in light of only one goal—altering current policy to achieve future fiscal solvency—because changes to the status quo are unavoidable under current projections. Achieving this goal is possible only through some combination of higher tax revenues and lower spending;[18] as demonstrated above, maintaining current policy through borrowing is unsustainable. In CBO's projection, Medicare and Medicaid spending grow continually relative to GDP. While clearly unrealistic as a "best guess" of future outcomes, it may make sense as a projection of current policy, for it underlines the fact that any policy changes to place the budget on a sustainable path must include reductions in the growth rate of government health spending.

Although the fiscal problems facing the government in the future are large, they are also distant. Budgetary resources are available for policy to continue along its current course for at least another decade or two. In this light, before evaluating specific reform proposals, it is useful to explore the arguments for not postponing reform further. Reforming now rather than later has been justified on at least three grounds: to reduce the scope of future policy changes, to improve inter-generational equity, and to reduce uncertainty.

Prefunding to Reduce the Scope of Policy Changes

One reason given to undertake reform today is to reduce the scope of the policy changes that must be ultimately undertaken. Reform, as defined in this chapter, reduces the government's overall future fiscal shortfall. Reforms made today can reduce the future fiscal shortfall without reducing the present fiscal shortfall. For example, a benefit cut could be announced today that did not go into effect until, say, 2030. But for reform to reduce the ultimate scope of future benefit cuts or tax increases, it must incorporate *prefunding—raising resources today and saving them so that more resources are available in the future to pay future benefits*. In other words, a smaller benefit cut could restore fiscal solvency if it went into effect today and its proceeds were saved than if it went into effect in 2030. For example, CBO estimates a fiscal gap (the immediate tax increases or spending cuts needed to stabilize the federal debt) of 8.1% of GDP over the next 75 years under current policy. Waiting until 2020 to change policy would increase the fiscal gap to 9.7% of GDP, and waiting until 2040 would increase it to 15.5% of GDP.

Prefunding can be done through the government (by paying down the national debt or investing the trust funds in private assets) or through individual accounts. The salutary effects of prefunding on the projected future fiscal imbalance are not limited to changes in Social Security and Medicare. Any policy change that reduced the current budget deficit would reduce the government's future fiscal gap; likewise, current budget deficits increase that fiscal gap. Prefunding increases the resources available to the government and economy as a whole by raising the national saving rate.[19] The additional saving is then available to finance additional capital investment spending (or reduce reliance on foreign saving to finance current investment), which increases national output. A greater national output increases the future resources available to finance the needs of an aging population, and reduces the government's fiscal shortfall.[20] The current fiscal stance of budget deficits, by contrast, eliminates the prefunding that would presently occur if the Social Security surpluses were saved and exacerbates the future fiscal shortfall for the same reasons. But making the transition to a prefunded system makes current generations worse off, because the prefunding must be financed either through higher taxes or lower benefits.

Prefunding requires higher revenues since under pay-as-you-go, existing revenues are already financing the benefits of current beneficiaries. (And because of the on-budget deficit, trust fund surpluses are already financing other government spending.) If reform were instead financed through borrowing, it would not improve the government's ability to pay benefits in the future (after adjusting for risk)—it would saddle future generations with explicit general government liabilities, in the form of a greater national debt. If reform is financed by borrowing, the increase in national saving in the trust fund or individual accounts is offset one for one by the decrease in government saving through the larger budget deficit.

Because benefits are tied to wages and GDP, prefunding not only increases the resources available to finance existing benefits promised by current law, it also increases the benefits themselves. (Prefunding leads to some fiscal improvement because it does not increase the Social Security benefits of those already retired.) To make prefunding a more effective strategy for improving future fiscal solvency, benefits could be de-linked from economic growth. De-linking Social Security benefits from economic growth is straightforward and can be accomplished by no longer tying benefits growth to wage growth. De-linking Medicare benefits from economic growth is less straightforward—as long as demand for health care increases with income, policies to increase GDP are also likely to increase the demand for Medicare spending.

Plans to reform through prefunding face a difficult political dilemma: how can a commitment to prefund be maintained and reform plans preserve a course of action that spans decades in the face of the comings and goings of new Congresses every two years? If reform plans cannot be preserved, little may be gained, from an economic perspective, by reforming now.[21] This is a particular concern since there could potentially be significant short-term political gains and few political costs from diverting prefunding resources to unrelated policy goals. History suggests that this concern is a real one: for example, the congressional "Social Security lock box" failed to prevent Social Security surpluses from being diverted to finance other spending beginning in 2001.[22] For this reason, prefunded individual accounts might have an important political advantage over centralized government prefunding because they take those resources "off the table" politically so that they could not be diverted to other uses. However, it is important to note that if individual accounts are debt-financed rather than prefunded, they will not be taking any resources "off the table."[23] Proponents argue that a centrally controlled trust fund invested in private assets would be another way to take those resources "off the table." Opponents argue that the earnings of a centrally controlled trust fund could be siphoned off to finance other government spending just as easily as the interest earnings of the trust funds are siphoned off today.

Inter-generational Equity

Another reason given for undertaking reform sooner rather than later is to pursue inter- generational equity. The choice for policymakers is whether to spread the tax increases or spending cuts over all generations beginning now through prefunding, or whether to concentrate the policy changes on future generations. Financing government spending through budget deficits does not impose less of a burden than tax increases or other spending cuts—it shifts the burden forward to future generations through a lower saving rate and capital stock.[24] The longer reform is postponed, the greater the benefit reductions or tax increases imposed on future generations. Economic theory cannot judge the desirability of a reform that shifted to prefunding because it is a question of inter-generational equity: is it "fair" that future generations are treated worse than current and past generations under current policy because of the effects of adverse demography on a pay-as-you-go system? Prefunding would place less of a burden on future generations, but would be unlikely to eliminate it since past generations received benefits that exceeded their contributions. Under current policy, the Trustees report for Social Security and Medicare estimated, respectively, that there will be a transfer of resources from future generations to past and present generations of workers equal to $16.3 trillion for Social Security and $14.2 trillion for Medicare in present value terms.[25] Some would argue that it is fairest to spread the unavoidable burdens of a pay-as-you-go system among all generations, rather than placing the entire burden on future generations. Others would argue that placing the burden on future generations is justified since they will be wealthier than current generations because of future economic growth. In the case of Medicare and Medicaid, another argument against current generations bearing more of the burden is the uncertainty about whether projected spending increases will actually materialize.

Deciding between benefit reductions and tax increases to restore future fiscal solvency is often viewed through the prism of fairness. This is somewhat misleading—in the aggregate, there is not much difference in fairness between cutting benefits and raising taxes on the same individual. For equity considerations, the generation affected by the reform is more important than the form that reform takes. Reforms undertaken now can raise taxes or lower benefits on current generations or future generations; reforms postponed to the future will only affect future generations. However, Social Security does provide favorable benefits to individuals who are low-income, widows, dependents, and the disabled, and maintaining the favorable treatment they currently receive would depend on the nature of the benefit cuts.

Reducing Uncertainty

Finally, another rationale for undertaking reform sooner rather than later is that it can reduce uncertainty. Workers trying to plan their optimum private saving behavior today are hampered by uncertainty concerning the benefits that will be provided by the government in the future. Some policy uncertainty is caused by the projected future fiscal shortfall, and can be reduced if the shortfall is reduced. On the other hand, there is forecast uncertainty, which complicates attempts to modify policy ahead of time, since policy responses could turn out to be larger or smaller than what turns out to have been needed. As demonstrated in **Figure 3**, the correct rate of future excess cost growth for Medicare and Medicaid is the largest source of long-term forecast uncertainty.

Uncertainty has implications for the types of reforms that can be undertaken. Policy options that affect individuals when they are old must be adopted far ahead of time if individuals are to be given time to adapt to those changes. For example, benefit cuts must be announced far in advance if individuals are to be given the opportunity to save more in their working years to offset benefit cuts. By contrast, policy options that affect individuals when they are young, such as tax increases, can be adopted more rapidly. This implies that postponing reform is likely to bias the eventual resolution toward tax increases rather than spending cuts.

Reform Options: Reducing Benefits

Social Security[26]

Relatively minor changes in benefit calculations could bring Social Security outlays back in line with revenues under the intermediate scenario.[27] For example, if initial benefits were indexed to price inflation instead of wage growth, outlays would fall significantly in the long run. If this were done, benefits would still be rising in nominal terms (and keeping constant in real terms), but the replacement rate of benefits compared to wages would fall. The advantage of this approach would be that savings to the government would rise over time (as the spread between wages and prices grew) to offset the increasing fiscal imbalance. (Since budgetary savings grow under this approach, larger reductions would be needed if postponed to the future.) A disadvantage of this proposal is that it is not directly tied to the size of the financial shortfall, so if the shortfall turned out to be smaller (larger) than expected, benefits would be cut more (less) than needed to restore solvency. CBO estimated that one proposal along these lines could reduce outlays under current policy to 4.1% of GDP from 5.8% of GDP by 2050.[28] This would keep Social Security spending near its current level as a share of GDP.

To avoid a reduction in their standard of living in retirement following a benefit cut, workers may choose to save more of their income during their working years or work longer. Thus, to the extent that Social Security substitutes for private saving, benefit cuts could lead to higher saving or labor supply which, in turn, would boost economic growth.[29] But to the extent that Social Security substitutes for family income transfers, households fail to plan ahead for retirement saving, or private saving is driven by other motives, such as a bequest motive or precautionary saving, reduced Social Security benefits would not influence private saving. Furthermore, the relatively unequal distribution of U.S. wealth suggests that private saving may not be that sensitive to changes in Social Security. At the top of the income distribution, which accounts for most U.S. saving, Social Security makes up little if any of an individual's retirement income. For example, elderly in the highest quartile of the income distribution received 20% of their income from Social Security in 2008.[30] At the bottom of the income distribution, a sizable fraction of Americans have very little private saving, and would presumably suffer a reduction in living standards rather than raise their saving rate in light of a benefit cut.[31]

An alternative approach to reducing benefits would be to raise the retirement and early retirement ages. This approach could avoid reducing monthly benefit payments, although lifetime benefits would fall since retirees would begin to collect benefits later in life. Proponents justify this approach on the grounds that rising life expectancy means that retirees are collecting benefits for longer than previous retirees—in effect, longer life expectancy has inadvertently caused lifetime benefits to increase. In addition, raising the retirement age would directly increase output by keeping workers in the labor force longer, thereby providing the economy as a whole with more resources to cope with an aging society. One study estimates that raising the retirement age to 70 would increase employment rates among men age 5 5-74 by as much as 15%, or total employment among men by 3%.[32] CBO estimated that a proposal to raise the retirement age and adjust early retirement benefits would reduce outlays in 2050 from a projected 5.8% of GDP under current policy to 5.0% of GDP.[33]

Medicare and Medicaid

Unlike Social Security, there are no straightforward proposals to reduce the long-term growth in Medicare and Medicaid spending. Social Security spending is based on specific formulas that can be altered to reach a desired spending level. Health spending, by contrast, is not currently set directly by the government. Rather, the government chooses the services it will finance, and the spending on those treatments ultimately depends on supply and demand. Little is known about how much long-term savings could be garnered from some of the proposals discussed below; it is likely that none of the proposals adopted in isolation could close the entire fiscal imbalance.[34] Restraining long-term health cost growth has been considered extensively in the 111th Congress's debate on health care reform, but to date CBO has concluded that the proposals would have a small effect on health spending relative to future budget deficits, and the budgetary savings generated would be at least partly offset by other parts of comprehensive reform bills that would tend to increase health spending.[35]

The central challenge for policymakers is to reduce excess cost growth. If spending on the health programs grew at the rate of GDP, they would not place a significant strain on government finances. However, there is no way to know what rate of excess cost growth will occur in the future. Forecasters assume that the rise in health spending will outpace GDP growth because it has consistently done so in the past. It is possible that technology or consumer preferences would change on their own such that excess cost growth wanes without government intervention. But it may be more prudent to assume that it will not wane, given historical patterns. Then the challenge becomes finding policy actions that can restrain excess cost growth.[36] Some economists argue that there are structural biases toward excess cost growth in the market for health care that could be altered by policymakers.

Policymakers can attempt to restrain cost growth through the demand side or supply side of the market. Demand could be reduced by shifting Medicare costs from the government to the beneficiaries, which would also directly reduce the government's fiscal gap and alter generational equity, if applied to current generations. (Shifting costs to the beneficiaries in the Medicaid program is arguably less philosophically compatible since it is a low-income support program.) Demand could be reduced by making beneficiaries bear a greater portion of Part B premiums.[37] (If desired, higher premiums could be means-tested to avoid negative effects on low-income individuals.) Beneficiaries currently pay about 25% of premiums and general revenues pay the remainder. However, higher premiums may have little effect on medical spending of participants (although it could reduce participation) since it would not influence the marginal cost of specific treatments (because premiums finance the overall insurance, not specific treatments). To influence marginal costs, raising deductibles and co-insurance rates would be more effective. But even if marginal costs were increased, some analysts are skeptical that consumers could make well-educated decisions based on price since choosing between medical procedures, unlike most goods, involves a highly specialized knowledge of medicine. And unless rules on supplemental coverage were altered, privately-purchased supplemental plans or Medicaid could cancel out policy changes that made marginal costs higher and shift health spending from Medicare to private spending and Medicaid.[38]

Another way to reduce demand would be to restrict enrollment. One way would be to raise the age of eligibility. In fact, unlike Social Security, Medicare's eligibility age is not already rising under current law. Modifying Medicare's eligibility age to match Social Security's would save billions of dollars, but the saving would still be modest in light of the program's future projected fiscal shortfall.[39]

Budgetary savings is not a rationale for reducing demand in and of itself. From an economic perspective, reducing demand is desirable if the benefits of receiving the health care are outweighed by the costs to society of their provision. Medicare may provide a service (elder health care) that could not be as efficiently provided by the market, notably because of adverse selection.[40] If higher costs to beneficiaries caused them to drop out of Part B or receive too little care (notably preventive care), Medicare spending could fall to a socially sub-optimal level. (Non-participation could be avoided by making participation mandatory, although this would increase budgetary pressures). On the other hand, since patients do not directly bear the costs, medical care may be over-consumed at present from a society-wide perspective, which would make a reduction in demand more economically efficient.

On the supply side of the market, spending could be reduced by restricting the medical services that the government will reimburse or limiting the coverage of newly developed treatments. Consequences of such an approach are that some medical spending would cease and some would be shifted to private spending and private insurance.

Some argue that another path to restraining cost growth lies with transforming Medicare from a government monopsony to a competitive market of private insurers, including the health maintenance organization (HMO) model that dominates employer-based coverage.[41] (This approach is sometimes referred to as "premium support.") The rationale behind this argument is that government lacks the profit-incentive, competitive pressures, and market savvy needed to restrain costs.

Others argue that government provision has two advantages over competition that make it more suitable. First, only government has monopsony bargaining power and economies of scale (which it does not fully use at present), and these can be used to hold down costs more effectively.[42] Second, an efficient insurance mechanism broadly pools risk so that the premiums of the healthy offset the costs of the sick. Health insurance could only be efficiently provided in competitive markets if adverse selection and cherry picking (private plans only serving healthy individuals to lower costs) could be avoided. Theoretically, adverse selection could be avoided through some combination of nondiscriminatory coverage, risk-adjusted premiums, and Medicare regulating the types of coverage that any plan must provide, but designing these tools effectively has been difficult in practice.[43] In any case, as an empirical matter, HMOs do not have a long enough track record to reach a consensus on whether they can reduce costs continually or only on a one-time basis. Although many analysts credit HMOs with reducing cost growth following their adoption in the 1990s, cost growth accelerated again in this decade.[44]

For the HMO model to reduce Medicare spending, it would have to be set up differently than the current Medicare Advantage system.[45] In the Medicare Advantage system, the government sets the minimum beneficiary premiums, the basic benefits offered, and the payments to companies. Thus, companies are not really free to compete on price, and efficiency gains cannot be translated into lower spending. Instead, companies compete on the medical services offered (they must offer a basket of services set by the government and can add additional services to that basket), so that, holding government-mandated premiums constant, efficiency gains are translated into higher profits or greater medical spending (because the company will offer the beneficiary more medical services). Preventing companies from competing on price is a way to reduce (but not likely eliminate) adverse selection; for companies to compete on price and the market to function efficiently, other tools would need to be found to prevent adverse selection.

Some analysts argue that reforms to Medicare's payment system could also generate cost savings. Health care providers are paid on a fee-for-service basis, which may give them an incentive to over-provide. Medicare payments are set by complex formulas that may not always match the price that Medicare could secure if bargained in the market. Once a treatment is approved by Medicare, the government leaves it to physicians, who have little incentive to consider the government's objective of limiting spending, to prescribe its use. Some researchers argue for "evidence-based medicine," claiming that cost-saving could be achieved by substituting less expensive treatments that are similarly effective.[46] For example, some researchers claim that the differences in outlays by region cannot be explained by cost of living and patient characteristics.[47] However, these types of reforms may lead to one-time, rather than continuous, cost savings.

Two other proposals to limit supply meet skepticism among economists. First, queuing (rationing under-supply through waiting lists) is widely used to reduce costs in foreign countries with nationalized health care systems. But economists are skeptical that the benefits of the lower financial costs exceed the nonfinancial costs of queuing. The nonfinancial cost can be thought of as the monetary price patients would be willing to pay to avoid the wait. Second, cutting Medicare's payments to providers cannot be used to restrain cost growth on an ongoing basis. While this strategy has been used in the past for short-term budgetary savings, to use it on an ongoing basis would require providers to accept continually lower payments for their services. Eventually, this would cause providers to withdraw their services, and some analysts have argued that this has occurred when payments have been cut in the past.

When evaluating all of the proposals made above, consider whether the goal of reform is to reduce federal spending or economy-wide spending on elderly health care. Answering this question is beyond the scope of this chapter, but many economists doubt that excess cost growth could be reduced in Medicare and Medicaid unless it is also reduced in private health care spending.[48] In other words, private corporations, insurers, and medical providers would have to change their behavior in order for health spending (and the budget) to be placed on a sustainable path. Some of these changes in private spending may come about through private sector initiatives and some through public policy changes. Many proposals could potentially replace Medicare spending with private spending, either by individuals or by the corporations from which they retired, or spending by state and local governments. Some proposals, adopted in isolation, would shift some spending from Medicare to Medicaid, which would limit the proposal's budgetary saving. Since Medicaid is a jointly funded state-federal program, there is frequently tension to shift costs back and forth between the two when either is looking to reduce overall spending.

Reform Options: Raising Taxes

The projected tax increases required to place Social Security back on a solvent financial path are not large compared with historical changes in tax revenues. If Social Security is maintained on a pay-as-you-go basis, tax increases of 1.2% of GDP are projected to be needed by 2050 (assuming, because of the overall budget shortfall, that general revenues are unavailable).[49] To place this total in perspective, tax revenues increased by 2.5 percentage points of GDP between 1993 and 1999, with little evidence of negative ramifications for the economy. If taxes are increased sooner and the revenues saved, the projected increase required to bring the system back to solvency is smaller.

Projected tax increases required to keep Medicare and Medicaid on sustainable paths and maintain benefits are much more daunting. Net spending on Medicare and Medicaid is projected to rise 7.8 percentage points of GDP by 2050. Gradual tax increases of these magnitudes need not be ruled out as infeasible since many Western European countries collect more than 50% of GDP in tax revenue, compared with 29% of GDP for the total of state, local, and federal government in the United States in 2007. Alternatively, if there were no excess cost growth, taxes would need to increase by 2 percentage points of GDP by 2050.

If reform relied on tax increases, what form could they take? Social Security and Medicare Part A are currently financed largely through payroll taxes, but could be financed in any way in the future (with or without a dedicated revenue source).

If taxes were levied on individuals, they could take the form of wage (payroll) taxes, income taxes, or consumption taxes. (If levied on corporations, other options would be available.) Tax revenue can also be raised at existing tax rates by broadening the tax base, an approach often favored by economists. Consumption and wage taxes affect labor supply but not saving decisions; income taxes affect both. Income taxes have a broader base and require lower tax rates in the long run. Wage or income tax increases could be made more progressive through a graduated rate structure; progressivity would be harder to achieve with consumption taxes. Consumption taxes would shift more of the burden of reform to the existing elderly because they tax existing saving when it is drawn down.

Besides tax rate increases, there could be changes made to the tax treatment of Social Security to raise revenue. For example, if policymakers wanted to make the system more progressive, the income ceiling on the payroll tax could be removed for Social Security (there is none for Medicare). Alternatively, Social Security benefits could be taxed in full (currently about two- thirds of recipients pay no tax on their benefits). (Whether these changes are consistent with the overall tax system depends if Social Security is viewed as a pension or income transfer system.) Revenues could be raised within Medicare through higher premiums for Parts B or D.

If the long-term fiscal imbalance were closed through higher taxes, raising taxes earlier and saving the proceeds through prefunding would require smaller tax increases than if tax increases were postponed. Earlier tax increases would be more economically efficient than larger increases later, and would affect generational equity by shifting some of the cost of reform to present generations. If taxes were raised today and the proceeds not saved, then the tax increases required in the future would not be reduced.

There is a widespread belief that lower spending is better for economic growth than higher taxes, but there is not strong evidence backing this belief. Economic theory is ambiguous as to the effects of higher taxes on growth in general, and it would also depend on what form the tax increase took. Either way, empirical evidence suggests that the economic effect is small for modest changes. In the case of closing the fiscal gap, however, the estimated changes are much larger. CBO estimates that eliminating the overall fiscal shortfall through higher marginal taxes would cause the economy to be 5% to 20% smaller in 2050 compared to if government spending were cut (under this projection, the economy would still be much larger than it is today).[50] CBO notes that there is little confidence surrounding these estimates since there is no comparable historical experience and little consensus over what model best describes how taxes affect the economy. Furthermore, CBO notes that the economic effects would be significantly smaller if revenue were raised by broadening the tax base instead of by raising marginal rates.

Taxes can affect economic growth by influencing labor supply (both the decision to work and the number of hours worked) or the saving rate. Empirical evidence is inconclusive as to the effects of taxes on saving because the decision to save is a very complicated one made over time and motivated by many different factors. Thus, results turn out to be highly sensitive to the model used. Currently, Social Security and Medicare Part A are financed by payroll taxes, which do not affect saving. However, even under the assumption that tax increases had no effect on the decision to save at the margin, raising taxes by several percentage points of GDP could reduce private saving by reducing after-tax income. Empirical evidence suggests that labor supply is relatively unresponsive to tax changes—most people, particularly men and single women, will work full-time regardless of tax rates.[51] In any case, individuals would not be expected to change their behavior as much in response to an increase in taxes for Social Security compared with a normal tax increase, because reducing labor supply would directly reduce the individual's benefits.

One demographic group whose labor supply may be more sensitive to tax rates is the elderly and near-elderly. This suggests that reform options that affect the (implicit or explicit) tax rate on the elderly could have important effects on the economy, even when those policies are intended to reduce entitlement spending. When entitlement spending is influenced by current income, spending policies can also act as a tax by reducing benefits when income rises.[52]

Some argue for reform based on tax increases on the grounds that recent tax cuts have contributed to the overall future shortfall between projected revenues and outlays. For example, the recent tax cuts, EGTRRA (P.L. 107-16 and JGTRRA (P.L. 108-27), have been estimated to increase the "fiscal gap," the long-term budget deficit, by 2.2% of GDP. To offset the effects of these tax cuts on the fiscal gap, an estimated 9% permanent reduction in all (noninterest) spending would be required.[53]

Reform Options: Individual Accounts

Individual accounts have been proposed as a potential solution to Social Security's financing problems.[54] Proponents argue that payroll tax revenues could be diverted to accounts that would be owned by the individual, and these accounts could be invested in financial securities. The high rate of return earned by the accounts, it is argued, could be used to reduce Social Security's fiscal shortfall.

Switching Social Security to a system of individual accounts, partially or completely, raises several economic issues that will not be addressed in this chapter, including questions of risk sharing, adverse selection, moral hazard, annuitization, and bequests.[55] Furthermore, individual accounts alone would not address the system's current social goals, which include redistribution and the provision of benefits for survivors, dependents, and the disabled, which currently accounted for approximately 3 7.6% of the system's outlays in 2008.[56] This chapter will only analyze the claim that individual accounts can improve the government's fiscal position.

As illustrated below, individual accounts would not be self-financing because savings to the government from the individual accounts would not occur until the account holders retire. All payroll tax revenues are currently dedicated to the payment of benefits to current retirees or the financing of general government spending—despite the Social Security surplus, there are no unused funds available to finance the creation of individual accounts. Thus, individual accounts would need to be financed by immediately raising taxes, reducing spending, or issuing Treasury securities (increasing the budget deficit); this is sometimes referred to as the "transition cost" of implementing individual accounts.[57]

Individual accounts are one vehicle through which prefunding can be implemented if financed through higher taxes or lower government spending. Then, all else equal, the government's overall fiscal position will improve, national saving will rise, private investment will increase, and this will increase the future size of the economy. [58] As noted above, individual accounts are not necessary for prefunding—prefunding can also occur if the government reduces the national debt or collectively invests in private securities. However, individual accounts may also be created without prefunding by increasing the size of the budget deficit.[59] If this occurs, no additional economic resources will be generated to reduce the government's fiscal imbalance. Any gain in government revenues from the individual accounts will in theory be offset by higher interest payments on the national debt (because the individual accounts were debt financed) and a lower rate of return earned by private investors (because the increased demand for private securities and government debt would push down the return on private securities and raise the interest rate that the government must pay to finance its debt). If individual accounts equal to 2%- 4% of payroll (0.8%-1 .6% of GDP) were introduced without a new source of revenue, as President Bush's Commission to Strengthen Social Security proposed in August 2001, the effect on interest rates and private rates of return could be significant. The creation of debt-financed individual accounts is a zero sum game for the economy as a whole because they do not raise the national saving rate (the rise in private saving is canceled by the decline in public saving) nor the national capital stock, all else equal, so they do not increase national income. Most proposals do not allow accounts to be "topped up" with voluntary private contributions, so there is little reason to think that the increase in private saving will exceed the decrease in private saving.[60]

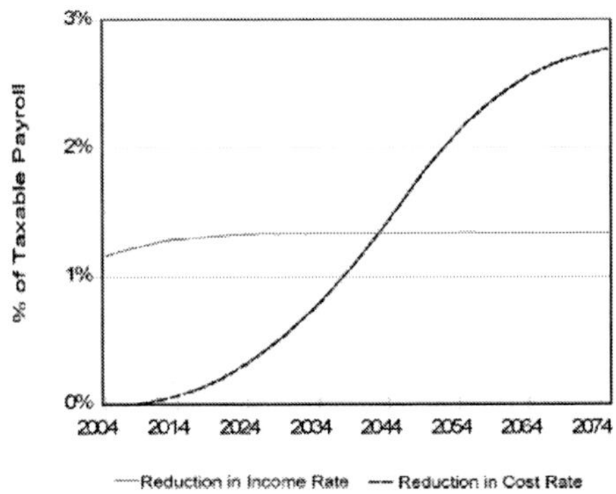

Source: Chief Actuaries of Social Security Administration, *Memorandum to President's Commission to Strengthen Social Security*, December 2001, p. 53.

Notes: Estimates based on Commission's Option 1 reform plan with 66.7% participation rate. It assumes accounts equal to 2% of payroll are introduced in 2004.

Figure 5. Change in Social Security's Finances From Introducing 2% Individual Accounts.

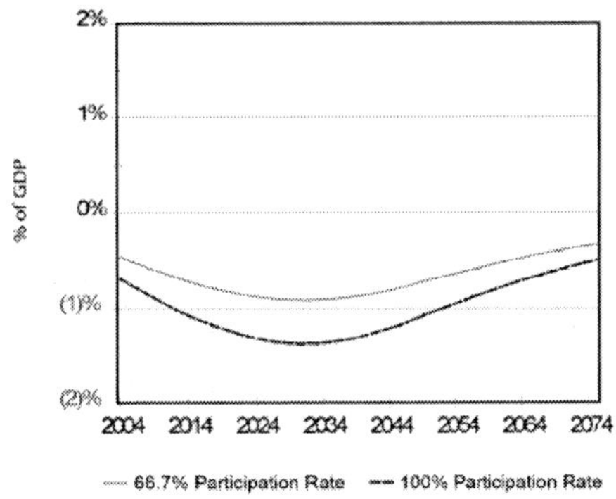

Source: Chief Actuaries of Social Security Administration, *Memorandum to President's Commission to Strengthen Social Security*, December 2001, pp. 5 3-54.

Note: Estimates based on Commission's Option 1 reform plan with 66.7% and 100% participation rate. It assumes accounts equal to 2% of payroll are introduced in 2004. Negative number signifies an increase in the deficit.

Figure 6. Change in Unified Budget Balance From Introducing 2% Debt-Financed Individual Accounts.

This argument can be made more concrete using official estimates provided by Social Security Administration actuaries of Option 1 in President Bush's Commission to Strengthen Social Security. In Option 1, workers under 55 could elect to deposit 2% of their OASDI taxable earnings in an individual account, with an offsetting reduction in benefits based on diverted amounts compounded at a real rate of return 3.5%, which is the source of budgetary saving to the government. Since Option 1 does not identify any new source of revenue to finance the accounts, they can be considered to be debt-financed. It is analyzed here because it is the only option that relies solely on individual accounts (Options 2 and 3 are a combination of individual accounts and benefit reductions.)

Figure 5 illustrates the *change* in the income and cost rates of the Social Security system as a percentage of taxable payroll caused by introducing individual accounts.[61] Diverting 2% of the payroll tax to individual accounts would reduce the income rate by an amount that would stabilize at about 1.33% of taxable payroll in a decade, assuming two-thirds of eligible workers participate. However, individual accounts would not lead to any significant decline in the cost rate for many years, since funds would not be withdrawn from individual accounts (which reduces the cost rate through the Social Security benefit offset) until they retire. The reduction in the cost rate steadily increases over time, approaching 2.75% of payroll in 2075, as larger individual accounts are amassed and then drawn down. For the first 40 years after the introduction of individual accounts, the accounts are projected to generate less revenue than was being diverted from beneficiaries. Roughly 40 years after the introduction of individual accounts, when enough retirees had spent their entire career making contributions, the reduction in benefits from the offset would exceed the revenue lost from a 2% marginal payroll tax cut. After that, the savings to the government would grow and eventually become large.[62]

Thus, individual accounts would exacerbate the financing problems of the Social Security system for roughly 40 years, but improve the system's finances from that point on. Whether this is desirable can only be determined by judging the effect of the accounts on the economy and government as a whole. Such accounts would improve the government's overall finances and national saving only if the revenue shortfalls caused by them in the first 40 years of their existence were financed through tax increases or benefit reductions.[63] By contrast, Figure 6 illustrates the projected *increase* in the unified budget deficit compared with current policy if the individual accounts are debt financed (i.e., introduced without an accompanying source of financing).[64] As explained above, the effect on the unified budget balance is the most meaningful measure because it is the only one that clearly identifies the cost of reform to the government as a whole.

Over the first 40 years of the accounts' existence, the decline in the income rate would exceed the decline in the cost rate, and the government would have to borrow the difference, increasing the national debt and interest payments on the debt. Once the decline in the cost rate exceeded the decline in the income rate, the effect of the individual accounts on the budget would be positive; however, this saving would be offset by the higher interest payments on the larger national debt. As long as the additional interest payments on the debt plus the decline in the income rate exceed the decline in the cost rate, the net effect of the individual accounts on the budget deficit would be negative. **Figure 6** indicates that individual accounts, if debt financed, *worsen the government's fiscal shortfall through 2075.*[65]

Because the private assets in individual accounts are growing through the accumulation of interest, these results may seem puzzling. Although the assets in individual accounts are growing, the debt issued by the government to finance the accounts is also growing because of interest accumulation. The individual accounts offset government benefits at a higher rate of return than the interest payments on government debt (3.0%), so eventually (outside the 75-year window) the individual accounts save the government money. (It is the benefit offset, not the earnings of the accounts, that reduce the government's liabilities.) But because so much debt must be issued immediately, it takes more than 75 years before the accounts pay for themselves. In fact, the actuaries of the SSA make two sets of assumptions, both of which are illustrated in Figure 6. Since the accounts are voluntary, they estimated the costs under the assumptions (1) that 66.7% of eligible individuals elect to participate, and (2) that 100% elect to participate. Comparing the results under the two assumptions leads to a result that may buck conventional wisdom: when individual accounts are debt financed, the cost to the government can be reduced by reducing the participation rate.

President Bush's Commission on Social Security made it clear that Option 1 would not avert a future financing crisis.[66] For that reason, it also proposed two further options that coupled the introduction of individual accounts with benefit reductions. But it follows from the data presented on Option 1, that it is only the benefit reductions, not the individual accounts (if debt financed) that improve the system's financial position in Options 2 and 3 through 2075.

Depending on the details, some individual account proposals could worsen the government's fiscal outlook by adding benefits or administrative costs to the current Social Security system. Many proposals allow the individual account's balance to be left as a bequest to heirs when the owner dies; when an individual (and, if applicable, his widow or her widower) dies prematurely in Social Security, the excess of taxes paid over benefits collected improves the system's financing. Individual accounts may require regulatory oversight financed from general revenues (e.g., to ensure that the accounts are not being invested fraudulently.) The government may feel obligated to "bail out" individual accounts with general revenue in the event of a stock market crash. Individual accounts may receive better or worse tax treatment than Social Security benefits, which would worsen or improve the government's finances, respectively. For example, 100% of withdrawals from traditional individual retirement accounts (IRAs) are taxed, while 0% to 85% of Social Security benefits are taxed (depending on income level). However, contributions to IRAs are deducted from taxable income, while the employee's half of Social Security contributions (payroll taxes) are not. If withdrawals from individual accounts receive the same tax treatment as IRAs, it would increase tax revenues; if contributions receive the tax treatment of IRAs, it would decrease revenues.

It should briefly be noted that the economic benefit of introducing individual accounts is unrelated to its effects on government finances. The economic benefit of individual accounts is that it could potentially lead workers to view Social Security less as a tax and benefit program and more as a pension. If so, it could reduce the distortions to work and save currently caused by Social Security. For example, workers may be more likely to continue working after they become eligible for retirement if they can continue accumulating contributions in their individual account, whereas the increase in Social Security benefits from working after normal retirement age are relatively small.[67] Whether these distortions are sizable, or even necessarily reduce growth, is an open question among economists. These economic benefits of switching to individual accounts would need to be weighed against the economic costs, which include problems of moral hazard, adverse selection, and less risk pooling.[68] If features are added to the accounts to reduce the economic costs, the economic benefits will also tend to be reduced.

Conclusion

The budget deficit reached 10% of GDP in 2009, an unsustainable level in the long run in the sense that it would cause the federal debt to continually grow faster than national income. While entitlement spending on the elderly had little to do with the recent increase in the deficit, it is the main reason why the deficit is projected to remain at high and rising levels in the long run under current policy. The retirement of the baby boomers, increased life expectancy, and the rising cost of health care are projected to make current policy unsustainable in the long run. Increases in spending are not expected to subside after the baby boomers have passed away. To keep the overall budget on a sustainable path over the next 50 years, either the projected rise in Social Security, Medicare, and Medicaid spending will have to be contained, or tax revenues will have to be increased, or both. Determining the right balance between benefit reductions or tax increases depends on people's desire to spend future income gains on health vs. non-health consumption expenditures, and whether those expenditures can be more efficiently and fairly supplied by the private sector or government programs. (Based on CBO projections, reduction in the growth of Medicare and Medicaid has to be part of the solution since it continually outpaces GDP growth.)

If current policy is maintained until 2030, CBO projects that some combination of tax increases and spending reductions totaling 12.1% of GDP would be needed at that point to place the budget on a sustainable path for the next 75 years. However, if reforms are made ahead of time, the ultimate size of required tax increases or benefit reductions could potentially be reduced. For example, CBO projects that immediate action would reduce the needed tax increases or benefit reductions to 8.1% of GDP. For this to occur, the revenues generated through tax increases or benefit cuts would have to be dedicated to a higher rate of public saving, thereby boosting economic growth. If the revenues are instead spent on other government spending or tax cuts, the ultimate size of future benefit cuts and tax increases will not have been reduced. Grappling with the fiscal solvency issue is also complicated by the inability to bind future Congresses to a longterm spending path—even if revenues raised are initially used to reduce the budget deficit, there is the risk that the fiscal improvement will be undone by future Congresses.

Determining how much benefits and revenues should be altered ahead of time is difficult, however, because of the wide degree of uncertainty associated with long-term government projections. In particular, if the projected future excess medical cost growth does not materialize, the budget outlook would dramatically improve. Crafting a solution to restore fiscal solvency faces the fundamental question of how much can be done at this point to prevent excess cost growth that has not yet happened—and may never happen. On the other hand, acting in advance may expand the array of feasible options. Restoring the system to solvency ahead of time would allow individuals enough forewarning that they could adjust to future benefit reductions without disrupting their spending patterns—for this reason, if reform is postponed, it is more likely to result in tax increases since notions of fairness make benefit cuts to those already retired unlikely.

What has already contributed to the fiscal imbalance is today's budget deficits, and the simplest and most concrete step that can be taken to reduce the fiscal gap is to reduce the current budget deficit. The salutary effects of prefunding on the future fiscal imbalance are not limited to changes in Social Security and Medicare. Any policy change that reduced the current budget deficit would reduce the government's future fiscal gap; likewise, current budget deficits increase that fiscal gap. The budget deficit in 2009 exceeded total net spending on Social Security, Medicare, and Medicaid—thus, placing the budget on a sustainable path in the near term cannot be accomplished solely through a focus on entitlement spending.

Social Security faces a financial imbalance that experts agree can be eliminated through relatively small increases in taxes and decreases in benefits,[69] and the changes could be minimized if they were prefunded today. The system faces no immediate financial shortfall—on the contrary, it is currently generating surpluses, so it is the only part of the budget that is not contributing to current budget deficits. It would not put pressure on the rest of the budget in its current state until at least 2016, according to the Social Security trustees. Individual accounts are not a substitute for benefit cuts or tax increases, although they could be a vehicle for either. Debt-financed individual accounts, by themselves, are projected to worsen the fiscal outlook over the next 75 years and not increase GDP through higher national saving.

Medicare and Medicaid face much larger and more intractable financial problems than Social Security. Historically, health care spending generally, and health care spending on the elderly in particular, have risen much more rapidly than has overall economic output. It is impossible to know if this pattern will continue in the future, but if it does, Medicare and Medicaid under current policy risk overwhelming budgetary resources. Yet unlike Social Security, spending on the health programs cannot be controlled directly unless access is restricted or rationed. To reduce future Medicare and Medicaid spending, the government must find a way to reduce the price or quantity of elderly health care provided. Quantity can be reduced either through restrictions on the medical treatments offered or by lowering demand. Demand could possibly be reduced through higher costs to the recipient, but the link between price and demand will always be indirect in an insurance program since marginal costs are largely borne by the insurer (in this case, largely the government), rather than the insured. Continually reducing prices on the supply side cannot be accomplished simply by continually reducing payments to providers. Ultimately, if payments decline and providers' costs do not, providers may stop offering those services. For that reason, many experts doubt that a reduction in Medicare and Medicaid cost growth can be sustained without a reduction in private health care cost growth. On the supply side, technological improvements or efficiency gains could in theory reduce future prices, although in recent years they have led to higher prices by making new (but expensive) treatments available. It is unclear what interventions government can pursue to reverse that trend. Certain modifications have been suggested that might lead to one-time efficiency gains, such as changes to the Medicare reimbursement system or the adoption of private sector HMO administration. But it is less clear that these modifications could lead to the continuous efficiency gains required to contain cost growth.

End Notes

[1] All projections in this chapter come from Congressional Budget Office, *The Long-Term Budget Outlook*, June 2009, unless otherwise noted. Similar projections can be found in Government Accountability Office, *The Nation's Long- Term Fiscal Outlook*, GAO-09-405SP, April 30, 2009; Office of Management and Budget, *Budget of the U.S. Government, Analytical Perspectives*, *Fiscal Year 2010*, May 2009, Ch. 13.

[2] Entitlement spending has risen over the past decade as the overall budget has shifted from surplus to deficit, but this rise in spending was anticipated and would not have been large enough to cause a budget deficit absent other policy changes. It was primarily those other policy changes, as well as a deterioration in economic conditions in the past year, that caused the budget to be in deficit when it had previously been projected to remain in surplus. For more information, see CRS Report R40435, *Budget Deficits: An Explanation of How Policy Affects Budget Balance*, by Mindy R. Levit and Marc Labonte.

[3] An exception is the portion of Medicare Part B which is financed through premiums paid by the elderly. About one quarter of Part B spending is paid through premiums and the other three quarters is paid by taxpayers, and can be considered to be financed on a pay-as-you-go basis. Part of Medicare Part D, the prescription drug benefit, will also be paid for by the elderly through premiums when implemented. A small fraction of Social Security's revenues also comes from the taxation of some Social Security benefits. Disability benefits are also part of the Social Security system.

[4] Data from Congressional Budget Office, *Long-Term Projections for Social Security: 2009 Update*, August 2009.

[5] Medicaid covers much long-term care spending and health spending for the lower-income elderly. CBO estimates that approximately 22% of all Medicaid spending is on the elderly.

[6] Glen Follette and Louise Sheiner, "The Sustainability of Health Spending Growth," Federal Reserve Board of Governors, *Finance and Economics Discussion Series 2005-60*, September 2005.

[7] The 2.5% excess cost growth assumption is included for illustrative purposes; as noted above, it is not possible for spending to rise that quickly over the projection window.

[8] Estimates of Medicaid spending presented here are for federal Medicaid spending only; state governments are also projected to see a large increase in future Medicaid spending. Estimates of Medicare spending are net of premiums paid by recipients.

[9] For more information, see CRS Report 94-486, *Supplemental Security Income (SSI): A Fact Sheet*, by Scott Szymendera.

[10] Sylvester Schieber and John Shoven, "The Consequences of Population Aging for Private Pension Fund Saving and Asset Markets," *The Economic Effects of Aging in the United States and Japan* (Chicago: University of Chicago Press, 1997), p. 111.

[11] Congressional Budget Office, *Federal Spending on the Elderly and Children*, July 2000.

[12] Withdrawals from tax-deferred saving vehicles have been projected to lead to only a small increase in revenues when the baby boomers retire, and may be more than offset by other factors that make revenues fall. Alan Auerbach, William Gale, and Peter Orszag, "Reassessing the Fiscal Gap: The Role of Tax-Deferred Saving," *Tax Notes*, July 28, 2003.

[13] Although some modest increase in the debt relative to GDP is sustainable, it is uncertain how much. Therefore, the fiscal gap assumption is a commonly used rule of thumb for estimating sustainability.

[14] See CRS Report RL3 1775, *Do Budget Deficits Push Up Interest Rates and Is This the Relevant Question?*, by Marc Labonte.

[15] See Henning Bohn, "Social Security Reform and Financial Markets," in Steven Sass and Robert Triest, eds., *Social Security Reform*, Federal Reserve Bank of Boston, Conference Series 41, June 1997, p. 196; John Geanakopolis, Olivia Mitchell, and Stephen Zeldes, "Social Security Money's Worth," NBER Working Paper 6722, September 1998.

[16] Congressional Budget Office, *Long-Term Projections for Social Security: 2009 Update*, August 2009; and The Board of Trustees of the Federal Hospital Insurance and Federal Supplementary Medical Insurance Trust Funds, *2009 Annual Report*, May 12, 2009.

[17] Some argue that the surpluses have created real resources because the government's unified budget deficit would have been even larger had it not been for the trust fund surpluses. This argument cannot be settled conclusively since there is no way of knowing the size of the unified budget deficit in the counterfactual case where there had not been Social Security surpluses. For a comparison of perspectives on the trust fund, see Kent Smetters, "Is The Social Security Trust Fund Worth Anything?," *National Bureau of Economic Research*, Working Paper 9845, July 2003.

[18] For an overview of Social Security reform and current legislation, see CRS Report RL33544, *Social Security Reform: Current Issues and Legislation*, by Dawn Nuschler.

[19] It should be noted that from an economic perspective, increasing resources available to the government is not important, since theoretically the government can raise taxes to any level they desire at any time. It is the increase in the resources of the economy that is important.

[20] See CRS Report RL30708, *Social Security, Saving, and the Economy*, by Brian W. Cashell

[21] Bosworth and Burtless present international evidence that saving in a public pension system is offset by dissaving in the rest of the government's budget. Barry Bosworth and Gary Burtless, "Pension Reform and Saving," working paper presented at the International Forum of Collaboration Projects, Tokyo, Japan, February 17-19, 2003.

[22] See CRS Report RS20165, *Social Security and Medicare "Lock Boxes"*, by David S. Koitz and Geoffrey C. Kollmann.

[23] Peter Diamond argues that these resources would not really be "off the table" because there would be political pressure to allow pre-retirement withdrawals from the accounts, as is allowed for individual retirement accounts (IRAs), and to substitute withdrawals from the accounts for government spending. See Peter Diamond, "Macroeconomic Aspects of Social Security Reform, *Brookings Papers on Economic Activity 2*, 1997, p. 1.

[24] See CRS Report RL30520, *The National Debt: Who Bears Its Burden?*, by Marc Labonte.

[25] The transfers could be considered underestimates because they do not include the $2.7 trillion combined trust fund assets that have been used to finance other government spending or the general revenue transfers to finance Parts B and D of Medicare equal to $18.7 trillion that financed the benefits of past and present generations. Some of these general revenues will be paid by future generations and some by present generations. See Tables III.C16 and III.C24 of the Medicare Trustees' Report and Table IV.B7 of the Social Security Trustees' Report.

[26] Proposed benefit reductions to close the fiscal gap are relative, not absolute, reductions. If future generations receive only the benefits that can be financed by dedicated revenues under current law, their dollar amount will still exceed the benefits paid to retirees today. However, these benefits will be lower relative to earnings because future earnings and life expectancy will be higher. (Likewise, tax increases would reduce after-tax income as a share of future income, but would still leave future citizens with higher incomes than today in absolute terms.) Similarly, under current law, even though the retirement age has increased, future retirees will spend more years in retirement collecting benefits than current retirees because of increases in life expectancy.

[27] The effect of a number of reform proposals on system solvency can be found in Social Security Advisory Board, *Why Action Should Be Taken Soon*, (Washington, DC: July 2001). The report also illustrates how much larger reforms would need to be if postponed.

[28] Congressional Budget Office, *Budget Options*, August 2009, p. 143.

[29] See Barry Bosworth and Gary Burtless, "Supply Side Consequences of Social Security Reform: Impacts on Saving and Employment," Center for Retirement Research at Boston College, Working Paper 2004-1, January 2004.

[30] CRS Report RL32697, *Income and Poverty Among Older Americans in 2008*, by Patrick Purcell.

[31] See James Poterba, "Discussion," in Steven Sass and Robert Triest, eds., *Social Security Reform*, Federal Reserve Bank of Boston, Conference Series 41, June 1997, p. 146. Data can be found in CRS Report RL32697, *Income and Poverty Among Older Americans in 2008*, by Patrick Purcell.

[32] See Barry Bosworth and Gary Burtless, "Supply Side Consequences of Social Security Reform: Impacts on Saving and Employment," Center for Retirement Research at Boston College, Working Paper 2004-1, January 2004, p. 38.

[33] Congressional Budget Office, *Budget Options*, August 2009, p. 145.

[34] Ten-year cost estimates for many Medicare reform proposals can be found in Congressional Budget Office, *Budget Options*, *Volume 1: Health Care*, December 2008.

[35] See, for example, Congressional Budget Office, *Patient Protection and Affordable Care Act, Incorporating the Manager's Amendment*, December 19, 2009. See also Congressional Budget Office, *Health Care Reform and the Budget*, June 16, 2009.

[36] There are conceptual difficulties with the idea that a policy change today can prevent excess cost growth from occurring over the next 75 years, when it is impossible to know whether it would have happened anyway. In this case, it would not be known if attempts to solve the problem had worked until well after the fact.

[37] Revenue estimates for raising premiums and other reform options can be found in Marilyn Moon, Misha Segal, and Randall Weiss, "A Moving Target: Financing Medicare for the Future," *Inquiry*, vol. 37, no. 4, Winter 2000/2001, p. 338. For example, the authors find that roughly quadrupling premiums in 2025 would raise government revenues by about 2% of GDP.

[38] See Government Accountability Office, *Medigap*, GAO-02-533T, March 14, 2002.

[39] See, for example, Congressional Budget Office, *Cost Estimate of S. 947/H.R. 2015 as passed by the Senate on June 25, 1997*, July 2, 1997. Because of changes to Medicare since this cost estimate was conducted, it should be viewed as giving only an order of magnitude estimate to the cost savings of the proposal.

[40] Adverse selection is caused by asymmetric information because patients know more about their health conditions (and therefore, potential medical costs) than insurers. Because of asymmetric information, sick patients will find an average price offered by insurers profitable and healthy patients will find it unfavorable. As a result, healthy patients could be driven out of the market, driving average prices up.

[41] Jonathan Oberlander, "Is Premium Support the Right Medicine for Medicare?," *Health Affairs*, vol. 19, no. 5, September/October 2000, p. 86.

[42] Health spending as a share of GDP has stabilized in the past few years in many advanced economies with government run single-payer health care systems. It is not clear that the policies responsible for this experience can be translated for the decentralized health sector of the United States. See Organization of Economic Cooperation and Development, *Health Data 2009*, July 1, 2009.

[43] As an example of how adverse selection may already affect Medicare, some analysts argue that HMOs providing Medicare+Choice plans are only profitable because they attract enrollees more healthy than the average but are paid by Medicare according to the average. See Barbara Cooper and Bruce Vladeck, "Bringing Competitive Pricing to Medicare," *Health Affairs*, vol. 19, no. 5, September/October 2000, p. 55.

[44] For example, see Marsha Gold, "Can Managed Care and Competition Control Medicare Costs?," *Health Affairs*, Web Exclusive, April 2, 2003.

[45] For more information, see CRS Report RL3261 8, *Medicare Advantage Payments*, by Paulette C. Morgan and Hinda Chaikind.

[46] For studies of variations in medical treatments and outcomes, see Dartmouth Atlas of Health Care, "Dartmouth Studies Show Wide Variation in Hospital Care and Outcomes For Chronically Ill Medicare Patients," press release, October 7, 2004.

[47] Uwe Reinhardt, "Health Care for the Aging Baby Boom: Lessons from Abroad," *Journal of Economic Perspectives*, vol. 14, no. 2, Spring 2000, p. 71.

[48] See, for example, Organization for Economic Cooperation and Development, *Economic Survey: United States*, vol. 2007/9, May 2007, ch. 3.

[49] Trustees of OASDI, *Annual Report, 2009*, Table VI.F4.

[50] Congressional Budget Office, "The Long-Term Economic Effects of Some Alternative Budget Policies," *Letter to the Honorable Paul Ryan*, May 19, 2008.

[51] See Theresa Devine, "Demographics, Social Security Reform, and Labor Supply" and Eric Engen and William Gale, "Effects of Social Security Reform on Private and National Saving," both in Steven Sass and Robert Triest, eds., *Social Security Reform*, Federal Reserve Bank of Boston Conference Series 41, June 1997, p. 77; Congressional Budget Office, *Labor Supply and Taxes*, memorandum, January 1996; Jerry Hausman, "Taxes and Labor Supply," Alan J. Auerbach and Martin Feldstein, eds., *Handbook of Public Economics*, vol. 1, New York, North Holland, 1985; CRS Report RL3 1949, *Issues in Dynamic Revenue Estimating*, by Jane G. Gravelle.

[52] For example, after a worker has accumulated 35 years of Social Security contributions, additional payroll taxes may exceed the further increases in benefits that they produce. Features of Social Security, Medicare, and tax policy like these cause the overall implicit "tax on work" after the age of 62 to far exceed the actual tax rate. One study shows that for a representative worker, the implicit marginal tax on work rises from 14.2% at age 55 to 24.7% at age 62 to 3 9.4% at age 65 to 49.5% at age 70. In other words, at age 70 a worker can only increase his after-tax and after-benefit spending by 50 cents for every dollar earned. These calculations are based on a representative worker who is a single male with a defined contribution pension. Women and married men with working spouses face somewhat lower implicit marginal tax rates. Barbara Butrica et al., "Does Work Pay at Older Ages?," Center for Retirement Research at Boston College, Working Paper 2004-31, November 2004.

[53] Alan Auerbach, William Gale, and Peter Orszag, "Sources of the Long-Term Fiscal Gap," *Tax Notes*, May 24, 2004, p. 1049.

[54] Similar proposals have been made by some for Medicare but have not received any congressional attention. See Martin Feldstein, "Prefunding Medicare," *National Bureau of Economic Research*, Working Paper 6917, January 1999. In his proposal, individual accounts would accumulate savings that could then be used to purchase health insurance upon retirement. See also Thomas Saving, "Making the Transition to Prepaid Medicare," *Journal of Economic Perspectives*, vol. 14, no. 2, Spring 2000, p. 85; and Laurence Seidman, "Prefunding Medicare Without Individual Accounts," *Health Affairs*, vol. 19, no. 5, September/October 2000, p. 72.

[55] These issued are comprehensively analyzed in CRS Report RL3 1498, *Social Security Reform: Economic Issues*, by Jane G. Gravelle and Marc Labonte.

[56] Trustees of OASDI, *Annual Report, 2009*, Table III.A5.

[57] See CRS Report RS22010, *Social Security: "Transition Costs"*, by Laura Haltzel.

[58] This assumes that the individual accounts are "carved out" of the existing Social Security system through benefit offsets and diverting some of the payroll tax. Some policymakers have instead recommended that the accounts be "added on" to Social Security by not altering present law benefits and not diverting the payroll tax. The effects of "add on" accounts on the economy are the same as "carve outs": if the accounts are financed through higher taxes or lower spending, then they will increase national saving (although less than one for one because there will be some offset in private saving), which will increase GDP. But if they are financed through larger budget deficits, they will not contribute to national saving, and therefore not increase GDP. However, no matter how they are financed, "add on" accounts do not reduce the government's fiscal gap because they do not reduce Social Security's liabilities nor introduce a new revenue stream that can be used to finance Social Security's liabilities.

[59] According to media reports, the Bush Administration stated that this was its plan at an economic summit in December 2004. Edmund Andrews, "Bush Puts Social Security at Top of Economic Conference," *New York Times*, December 15, 2004.

[60] Since the individual accounts do not reduce the government's fiscal gap, individuals with "rational expectations" would not be expected to respond to the creation of the accounts by reducing their private saving. Nevertheless, if individuals perceived the individual accounts as new net wealth to them, they might decide that they need to save less to meet their retirement needs.

[61] The income rate refers to payroll tax revenue collected by the Social Security system. The cost rate refers to the benefits paid by the Social Security system. Taxable payroll is the tax base from which payroll revenues are collected.

[62] Since the graph shows the *change* in the income and cost rates caused by introducing individual accounts, a future financing crisis is averted only if the proposals generate enough additional revenues to cover the entire financing gap.

[63] The accounts are unlikely to raise private saving by more than the fall in public saving, since the accounts come from tax revenue and cannot be supplemented by private saving contributions.

[64] This graph does not illustrate the overall budget deficit under a system of individual accounts, but rather the *change* in the budget deficit caused by the introduction of individual accounts.

[65] At some point beyond the 75-year projection window, the effect of introducing debt-financed individual accounts on the budget deficit may turn positive, but projections of a long enough duration to answer that question are not available.

[66] President's Commission to Strengthen Social Security, *Final Report*, December 2001, p. 15.

[67] Barry Bosworth and Gary Burtless, "Supply Side Consequences of Social Security Reform: Impacts on Saving and Employment," Center for Retirement Research at Boston College, Working Paper 2004-1, January 2004.

[68] The economic costs and benefits of the current system compared with a system of individual accounts are analyzed in CRS Report RL3 1498, *Social Security Reform: Economic Issues*, by Jane G. Gravelle and Marc Labonte.

[69] For examples of specific proposals, see Peter Diamond and Peter Orszag, *Saving Social Security* (Washington, DC: Brookings Institution Press, 2004).

In: The Long-Term Budget Outlook
Editor: Jessica C. Anderson
ISBN: 978-1-61122-190-9

Chapter 3

IMPACT ON THE FEDERAL BUDGET OF FREEZING NON-SECURITY DISCRETIONARY SPENDING

Mindy R. Levit

SUMMARY

As economic recovery continues, the focus on the federal budget has shifted, in part, towards deficit reduction. In fiscal year (FY) 2009, the federal budget deficit, relative to the size of the economy, reached a level not seen since the end of World War II. Deficit levels are projected to remain elevated through FY2011. The budget deficit for FY2011, according to CBO's analysis of the President's budget, is projected to be $1,342 billion. In his FY2011 budget, the President made several proposals to curb spending, while acknowledging that additional steps are needed to achieve long-term fiscal stability.

The President proposes to freeze non-security discretionary spending for the next three fiscal years (FY2011-FY2013) at FY2010 nominal levels (i.e., spending levels would not be adjusted for inflation). After FY2013, growth in this category of spending would be linked to inflation. Non-security discretionary spending is defined as discretionary spending outside of defense, homeland security, veterans affairs, and international affairs. If enacted in this form, the President's budget projects that this proposal would save approximately $250 billion over the next 10 years.

Under the Administration's Current Policy baseline, the deficit is projected to equal 7.5% of GDP in FY2011, falling to 5.6% of GDP in FY2020. If all of the President's proposed policies are implemented, the Administration projects that the deficit will fall from 8.3% of GDP in FY2011 to 4.2% of GDP in FY2020. In other words, the deficit would be 1.4% of GDP lower in FY2020 compared to current policy if all of the President's proposals are enacted. In order to achieve even greater deficit reduction, larger cuts would be needed. To illustrate, even if non-security discretionary spending is cut to zero and there are no other policy changes implemented, the deficit would fall from 4.0% of GDP in FY2011 to 3.3% of GDP in FY2020. This would mean no federal funding for education, transportation, most energy, and numerous other programs. In order to balance the budget, significant additional spending cuts, tax increases, or a combination would still be required.

Freezing non-security discretionary spending can reduce the deficit relative to certain policy alternatives. In other words, whether or not freezing non-security discretionary spending actually lowers the deficit depends on which deficit projections are used as the starting point to measure the impact of policy changes. Depending on which one of the three Administration's baseline scenarios are used as a starting point to measure savings, this proposal may generate lower levels of savings compared to what is described in the President's budget. Achieving savings from this proposal ultimately depends on what policies Congress enacts this year and in each subsequent budget cycle. Congress enacts appropriations every year and would continue to face a decision on legislation restraining non-security discretionary spending in future years.

The proposal to place a three-year freeze on non-security discretionary spending, as analyzed in this chapter, represents a small reduction in the federal budget deficit. Freezing this spending does not address longer-term budgetary challenges.

As economic recovery continues, the focus on the federal budget has shifted, in part, towards deficit reduction. In fiscal year (FY) 2009, the federal budget deficit, relative to the size of the economy, reached a level not seen since the end of World War II. Deficit levels are projected to remain elevated through FY2011. The budget deficit for FY2011, according to CBO's analysis of the President's budget, is projected to be $1,342 billion.[1] As concern over the long-term effects of an elevated federal budget deficit grows, the

President's FY2011 budget contains several proposals intended to reduce the deficit to more sustainable levels.[2]

In his FY2011 budget proposal, the President made several proposals to immediately curb spending, while acknowledging that additional steps are needed to achieve long-term fiscal stability. The President's budget proposes a three-year freeze on non-security discretionary spending, along with other specific programmatic terminations and reductions. The budget also includes a recommitment to cut the deficit in half by the end of the President's current term, with the ultimate objective of enacting policies to achieve a sustainable budget deficit. To assist in reaching this goal, the President created a fiscal commission tasked with providing recommendations to balance the budget, exclusive of interest payments, by FY2015.

This chapter examines the impact on the federal budget of the President's proposals, specifically the proposed freeze in non-security discretionary spending and how the freeze might change the fiscal outlook over the 10-year budget window.

THE PRESIDENT'S PROPOSALS

Non-Security Discretionary Spending Freeze

The President proposes to freeze non-security discretionary spending for the next three fiscal years (FY2011-FY2013) at FY2010 nominal levels (i.e., spending levels will not be adjusted for inflation). After FY2013, growth in this category of spending would be linked to inflation.[3] If enacted in this form, the President's budget projects that this proposal will save approximately $250 billion over the next 10 years, relative to current policy.[4]

Non-security discretionary spending in this proposal is defined as discretionary budgetary resources outside of defense, homeland security, veterans affairs, and international affairs.[5]

Non-security discretionary budgetary resources include budget authority for non-security federal departments and agencies as well as the obligation limitations of the Department of Transportation, provided every year through the appropriations process.[6]

The freeze in non-security discretionary budgetary resources does not impact all programs and agencies uniformly. For example, funding is proposed to be eliminated or consolidated in several education programs, while others receive funding increases.[7] There are proposals to increase government-wide spending for job training and employment programs. Spending increases for research and development funding will be targeted to the National Science Foundation, the Department of Energy's Office of Science, and the National Institute of Standards and Technology, while the President's budget would cancel NASA's Constellation program.[8]

At the agency level, the largest cuts in budgetary resources are proposed for the Department of Commerce ($5 billion), the Department of Justice ($3.4 billion), and the Department of Housing and Urban Development ($2 billion). Those entities receiving the largest increases include the Department of Education ($2.9 billion), the Department of Transportation ($1 billion), and the Social Security Administration ($0.8 billion).[9]

Other Savings Proposals

Two other major savings proposals accompanied the President's budget. They include the FY2011 Terminations, Reductions, and Savings (TRS) budget volume, and the creation of a fiscal commission tasked with providing policy recommendations to achieve long-run fiscal stability. In the TRS volume, 78 discretionary programs are listed for termination or reduction, yielding savings of $10 billion in FY2011.[10] In addition, the President proposes to terminate or reduce spending for 33 mandatory programs, saving $240 billion over 10 years.

For FY2010, Congress approved nearly 60% (or $6.8 billion) of the discretionary spending cuts proposed in that year's Terminations, Reductions, and Savings budget volume.[11] However, some of the FY2011 terminations and reductions are similar to those proposed but not accepted by Congress for FY2010, which may indicate that it will be harder to gain approval for these cuts, which were already previously rejected.

To meet the Administration's proposal to freeze non-security discretionary spending Congress may need to accept many or all of the proposed terminations and reductions. If Congress accepts all of the proposed cuts, the savings for FY2011 alone would amount to roughly $21.4 billion for mandatory and discretionary programs.

Table 1. Proposed Discretionary Budgetary Resources by Fiscal Year Billions of Dollars.

	2010[a]	2011	2012	2013	2014	2015	2016	2017	2018	2019	2020
Security	855	879	798	849	840	864	885	907	929	953	978
Non-Security	447	441	446	446	459	472	479	489	502	517	538
Percentage change from prior year in non-security discrete-onary spending	—	-1.1%	1.2%	0.0%	2.9%	2.9%	1.4%	2.1%	2.6%	3.1%	4.0%
Total discretionary	1,302	1,320	1,244	1,265	1,299	1,336	1,363	1,395	1,431	1,470	1,515
Non-security spend-ing as a percentage of total discretionary spending	34.3%	33.4%	35.9%	35.3%	35.3%	35.3%	35.1%	35.1%	35.1%	35.2%	35.5%

Source: CRS calculations based on U.S. Office of Management and Budget, *Budget of the U.S. Government: Fiscal Year 2011*, Tables S-4, S-10, and S-11.

Notes: The Administration defines budgetary resources as budget authority plus "obligation limitations" for the Department of Transportation. Totals may not add due to rounding.

[a].Includes $41 billion in proposed supplemental funding not yet enacted.

The Administration hopes to achieve additional savings by working with Congress to enact forthcoming recommendations of the fiscal commission, which was created by executive order on February 18, 2010. The commission's task is to balance the budget, excluding net interest payments, by FY2015. The commission's recommendations would lead to annual budget deficits of roughly 3% of GDP, equal to the projected amount of interest payments in FY2015. The recommendations of the commission must be submitted to Congress by December 1, 2010, with 14 out of 18 members, according to the executive order, needing to vote to report the recommendations.[12]

TRENDS IN NON-SECURITY DISCRETIONARY BUDGETARY RESOURCES

Table 1 shows the proposed levels of discretionary budgetary resources from FY2010 through FY2020, broken out by security and non-security discretionary spending. Also included are (1) the percentage increases or decreases relative to the prior year's levels of non-security discretionary budgetary resources, and (2) non-security discretionary budgetary resources as a percentage of total discretionary budgetary resources.

According to these figures in the President's budget, non-security discretionary spending, as measured by budgetary resources, is estimated to fall by 1.1% from FY2010 to FY2011. Spending will rise by 1.2% between FY2011 and FY2012 and will remain flat between FY2012 and FY2013. Between FY2014 and FY2020, non-security discretionary spending is projected to rise 2.7% per year, on average. Over the FY2010 to FY2020 period, non-security discretionary spending is expected to average 35% of total discretionary budgetary resources and approximately 12% of total budgetary resources, representing a relatively small portion of total government spending.[13]

Discretionary spending comprises a relatively small portion of total spending. In FY1 970, the federal government spent nearly 62% of total outlays on discretionary spending, 31% of total outlays on mandatory programs, and 7% of total outlays on net interest payments. While the composition of spending has fluctuated over time, larger trends show a reversal in total outlays dedicated to mandatory and discretionary spending.[14] In the most recently completed fiscal year, FY2009, the federal government spent 35%, 60%, and 5% of total outlays on discretionary spending, mandatory programs, and net interest payments, respectively. The amount of federal funds spent on discretionary programs in FY2009 is nearly equivalent, as a percentage of total outlays, to the amount spent on mandatory spending in FY1970. Cutting discretionary programs will generate smaller effects on the overall budget picture compared to reducing other types of spending, all else equal.

Typically, discretionary spending is divided into defense and non-defense categories (rather than security and non-security).[15] Between FY2001 and FY2010 (estimated), non-defense discretionary budget authority has risen 5.3% per year on average.[16] Considering the rapid growth in this type of spending over the last decade, it may be challenging to enact the President's proposal to freeze a large portion of this spending over the next three fiscal years.

ILLUSTRATING THE IMPACT OF THE PRESIDENT'S PROPOSAL TO FREEZE NON-SECURITY DISCRETIONARY SPENDING

To illustrate the impact of the policies proposed in the FY2011 budget, the Administration computes three budget baselines. The purpose of a baseline is to provide a starting point from which to measure the costs or savings of policy proposals. First, it projected a Budget Enforcement Act (BEA) baseline, using methods that mirror those that CBO uses to project its current-law baseline. This projection assumes, among other things, that discretionary spending remains constant in real (i.e., inflation-adjusted) terms. This methodology for computing the baseline has received some criticism because it does not take into account expiring policies, which are likely to be extended as they have been in past years. This results in a budget outlook that is generally considered more favorable than what is likely to occur. The second set of projections, the Current Policy baseline, assumes that certain policies due to expire will be continued. The President's Budget views the Current Policy baseline as the most realistic projection of the budget deficit and is used as their benchmark to measure the impact of their proposals. The final deficit projection, the Proposed Budget baseline, illustrates the impact if all of the policies proposed by the President were implemented. Generally, the deficit levels in the Proposed Budget scenario fall between the lower BEA baseline and the higher Current Policy figures.[17]

The spending controls proposed in the President's FY2011 budget do not directly result in cuts in deficit levels. That is because outlays, not budgetary resources as the Administration proposes to freeze, are used to calculate the budget deficit and are what would ultimately measure the savings generated by the proposal. Budget authority from a single year can result in outlays in multiple years. Though the proposed freeze in non-security discretionary budgetary resources only extends for the next three fiscal years and is followed by spending growth linked to inflation thereafter, outlay savings are projected over the entire FY2011-FY2020 period relative to Current Policy.

Table 2 shows the effect on the deficit resulting from the non-security discretionary spending freeze and from the other policy proposals in the President's budget. In FY2011, the proposal to freeze non-discretionary spending results in a small budgetary savings of $10 billion. However, the other proposals in the President's budget would result in an overall increase in the deficit relative to the Current Policy baseline. Over the FY2011 -FY2020 period, the freeze in non- security discretionary spending would achieve budgetary savings of $25 billion, on average, in each fiscal year. With a cumulative budget deficit of $10,640 billion over the 10-year period if current policies continue unchanged, the $249 billion in savings generated from the non-security discretionary spending would result in a 2.3% reduction in the deficit.

To further illustrate the impact on the federal budget deficit of freezing non-security discretionary budgetary resources, it is useful to analyze the savings from this proposal relative to savings that could be generated if other types of spending cuts are enacted. **Table 3** illustrates the impact that different policy scenarios could have on the budget deficit over the next 10 years. The scenarios and resulting deficit projections shown in the table are (1) the President's Current Policy baseline, (2) the President's Current Policy baseline with non-security discretionary budgetary resources frozen, (3) the President's Proposed Budget baseline (which includes the freeze in non-security discretionary budgetary resources as well as all other proposals), (4) CBO's analysis of the President's Proposed Budget, and (5) the President's Current Policy baseline with non-security discretionary spending cut to zero.

Table 2. Budgetary Savings of President's Proposals by Fiscal Year Deficit increase (+) or decrease (-) in Billions of Dollars.

	2011	2012	2013	2014	2015	2016	2017	2018	2019	2020	2011 - 2020
Budget deficit under "Current Policy"	1,145	934	940	934	983	1,013	1,042	1,077	1,227	1,346	10,640
From freezing non-security discretionary budgetary resources	-10	-15	-24	-27	-29	-29	-30	-31	-30	-25	-249
From all other proposed policy changes	131	-90	-189	-201	-202	-206	-234	-261	-289	-318	-1,859
Budget deficit under "proposed policy"	1,267	828	727	706	752	778	778	785	908	1,003	8,532

Source: U.S. Office of Management and Budget, *Budget of the U.S. Government: Fiscal Year 2011*, Table S-2.

Notes: The budgetary savings from these proposals are relative to the Administration's baseline projections of "Current Policy," which include an extension of the AMT patch and the 2001 and 2003 tax cuts, an increase in Medicare physician payments, and several other policies. Totals may not add due to rounding.

Under the Current Policy baseline, the deficit is projected to equal 7.5% of GDP in FY2011, falling to 5.6% of GDP in FY2020. Using the Current Policy baseline as a starting point, enacting only the freeze in non-security discretionary budgetary resources as proposed by the President would result in a FY2011 deficit of 7.4% of GDP and 5.5% of GDP in FY2020. In contrast, if all of the President's proposed policies are implemented, the Administration projects that the deficit will fall from 8.3% of GDP in FY2011 to 4.2% of GDP in FY2020. In other words, the deficit would be 1.4% of GDP lower in FY2020 compared to current policy if all of the President's proposals are enacted. Under CBO's projections of the Administration's proposed budget, the deficit is projected to fall from 8.9% of GDP in FY2011 to 5.6% of GDP in FY2020.[18] While falling under all of these scenarios during the middle of the 10-year budget window, the budget deficit is expected to begin an upward trajectory in the final fiscal years of this period.

These scenarios indicate that in order to achieve greater deficit reduction, larger cuts would be needed. For purposes of illustrating the levels of spending cuts that would be required to come closer to achieving a more sustainable budget deficit, **Table 3** also shows discretionary spending and deficit levels if non-security discretionary spending is cut to zero.[19] This scenario would mean no federal funding for education, transportation, most energy, and numerous other programs. Using the Current Policy baseline as a starting point, if non-security discretionary spending was cut to zero and no other policy changes were implemented, the deficit would fall from 4.0% of GDP in FY2011 to 3.3% of GDP in FY2020. This scenario illustrates that to achieve a sustainable budget deficit, additional spending cuts, tax increases, or a combination would still be required.

Does Cutting Non-Security Discretionary Spending Really Lower the Deficit?

Freezing non-security discretionary spending can reduce the deficit relative to certain policy alternatives. In other words, whether or not freezing non-security discretionary spending actually lowers the deficit depends on which deficit projections are used as the starting point to measure the impact of policy changes. As described earlier, the President's budget contains three budget scenarios, the BEA baseline, the Current Policy baseline, and the Proposed Policy baseline. To measure the savings generated by the proposed freeze in non-security discretionary spending, the Administration measured discretionary spending against the Current Policy baseline, which generates total savings of $250 billion over the FY2011 -FY2020 period. Depending on which baseline scenario is used as a starting point, this proposal may generate lower levels of savings compared to what is described in the President's budget. For example, if one considered any growth in discretionary spending to be an increase over current policy, the proposal would yield no savings.

Some of the funding cuts proposed to achieve this freeze would likely have occurred anyway. Funding for the Department of Commerce's Census Bureau is proposed to fall by nearly $6 billion between FY2010 and FY2011, from $7.2 billion in FY2010 to $1.3 billion in FY2011. The Census Bureau received a large boost in funding in FY20 10 to conduct the decennial census, with some funds remaining available though FY2011.[20] Other bureaus within Commerce would receive increases in funding as the overall cut for the department amounts to $5 billion. The proposed cut in funding for the Department of Commerce is the largest of any agency or program between FY2010 and FY2011, and represents nearly all of the savings in budgetary resources between FY2010 and FY2011.[21]

As shown in **Table 1**, despite the drop in non-security discretionary budgetary resources between FY20 10 and FY2011, from $446.7 billion to $441.3 billion, spending rises again between FY2011 and FY2012, from $441.3 billion to $446.4 billion, and remains flat in FY20 13, at $446.2 billion. While the FY2012 and FY2013 levels are essentially equal to the FY20 0 level, this funding freeze is based on elevated non-security discretionary budgetary resources from the American Recovery and Reinvestment Act (ARRA, P.L. 111-5). CBO's cost estimate showed that most of the discretionary budget authority from ARRA was available in FY2009, with another $7.1 billion slated to be available in FY2010.[22] The freeze in non-security discretionary spending, based on FY20 10 levels, therefore contains at least some funding meant to be one-time spending.

While the Administration wants to limit non-security discretionary spending over the next 10 years, proposed security discretionary spending levels rise over the next decade. Increased security spending is expected in increase the deficit by $284 billion between FY2011 and FY2020. Excluding the costs of overseas contingency operations, total discretionary spending is projected to rise by $35 billion between FY2011 and FY2020.

Table 3. Budget Deficit Effects of Changing Discretionary Spending Levels FY20 1 1-FY2020.

2011		2012	2013	2014	2015	2016	2017	2018	2019	2020
Discretionary Spending Levels (outlays, in billions of dollars):										
Current Policy baseline	1,376	1,340	1,343	1,367	1,396	1,425	1,460	1,496	1,534	1,573
Current Policy baseline with non-security discretionary spending frozen	1,366	1,325	1,319	1,339	1,368	1,396	1,430	1,465	1,504	1,548
President's Proposed Budget (including non-security discretionary spending freeze)	1,415	1,301	1,267	1,283	1,310	1,337	1,371	1,405	1,442	1,484
CBO analysis of Pres. Proposed Budget (including non-security discretionary spending freeze)	1,401	1,334	1,301	1,303	1,323	1,355	1,381	1,407	1,446	1,487
Current Policy baseline with non-security discretionary cut to zero	846	850	863	882	903	921	944	968	993	1,019
Budget Deficit (as a percentage of GDP):										
Current Policy baseline	7.5%	5.8%	5.5%	5.1%	5.1%	5.0%	4.9%	4.9%	5.3%	5.6%
Current Policy baseline with non-security discretionary spending frozen	7.4%	5.7%	5.3%	5.0%	5.0%	4.9%	4.8%	4.7%	5.2%	5.5%
Pres. Proposed Budget (including non-security discretionary spending freeze)	8.3%	5.1%	4.2%	3.9%	3.9%	3.9%	3.7%	3.6%	3.9%	4.2%
CBO analysis of Pres. Proposed Budget (including non-security discretionary spending freeze)	8.9%	5.8%	4.5%	4.1%	4.3%	4.7%	4.7%	4.8%	5.3%	5.6%
Current Policy baseline with non-security discretionary cut to zero	4.0%	2.7%	2.7%	2.5%	2.6%	2.5%	2.5%	2.5%	3.0%	3.3%

Source: U.S. Office of Management and Budget, *Budget of the U.S. Government: Fiscal Year 2011*, Table S-1. CRS calculations based on U.S. Office of Management and Budget, *Budget of the U.S. Government: Fiscal Year 2011*, Tables S-1 and S-4 and U.S. Congressional Budget Office, *An Analysis of the President's Budgetary Proposals for Fiscal Year 2011*, Table 1-2.

Notes: In the deficit estimates under the scenarios of the President's Current Policy baseline with non-security discretionary spending frozen and cut to zero, net interest savings are not included. CBO and OMB have different assumptions about economic growth projections.

Finally, achieving savings from this proposal ultimately depends on what policies Congress enacts this year and in each subsequent budget cycle. Even if Congress does enact the President's proposal to freeze non-security discretionary spending in this year's budget, it is hard to bind future Congresses to freeze this spending in later periods. Because Congress enacts appropriations every year, it would continue to face a decision on legislation restraining non- security discretionary spending in future years as well.

End Notes

[1] U.S. Congressional Budget Office, *An Analysis of the President's Budgetary Proposals for Fiscal Year 2011*, March 2010, Table 1-2, available at*http://www.cbo.gov/ftpdocs/112xx/doc11280/03-24-apb.pdf.*

[2] For a full analysis of the FY2011 federal budget, see CRS Report R41097, *The FY2011 Federal Budget*, by Mindy R. Levit.

[3] U.S. Department of the Treasury, Treasury Secretary Timothy F. Geithner, written testimony, p. 7, for U.S. Senate Budget Committee, February 4, 2010, available at *http://budget.senate.gov/democratic/testimony/2010/*TG_Budget%20Testimony_SBC.pdf.

[4] U.S. Office of Management and Budget, *Budget of the U.S. Government, Fiscal Year 2011, Budget Volume*, Table S2.

[5] U.S. Office of Management and Budget, *Testimony of Peter R. Orszag, Director of the Office of Management and Budget*, p. 7, before the U.S. Senate Budget Committee, February 2, 2010, available at http://www.whitehouse.gov/ omb/assets/testimony/orszag_budget_020210.pdf.

[6] The obligation limitations for the Department of Transportation (DOT) are derived from the contract authority of Highway and Aviation Trust Funds. Contract authority is a type of budget authority that is available for obligation as a result of provisions in authorizing legislation, without requiring any further legislative action (i.e., without any appropriation by Congress). In order to impose a limit on the amount of money that the government can be obligated to spend on federal highway and aviation programs financed through the DOT's trust funds, the amount of contract authority that can be obligated is limited by a spending control mechanism called a "limitation on obligations" (often referred to as "ObLim" or "Oblimit"). The ObLim for each year is set in the authorizing legislation, and is included in the DOT appropriations bill. For more information, see CRS Report R40053, *Surface Transportation Program Reauthorization Issues for the 111*th *Congress*, coordinated by John W. Fischer; CRS Report RL33913, *Aviation Finance: Federal Aviation Administration (FAA) Reauthorization and Related Issues*, by John W. Fischer; and CRS Report R40805, *Transportation, Housing and Urban Development, and Related Agencies (THUD): FY2010 Appropriations*, by David Randall Peterman and Maggie McCarty.

[7] U.S. Department of the Treasury, Treasury Secretary Timothy F. Geithner, written testimony, p. 7, for U.S. Senate Budget Committee, February 4, 2010.

[8] U.S. Office of Management and Budget, *Testimony of Peter R. Orszag, Director of the Office of Management and Budget*, p. 7, before the U.S. Senate Budget Committee, February 2, 2010.

[9] Proposed increases in discretionary budget authority do not include the following: (1) Department of Education— does not account for Pell Grant funding; (2) Department of Transportation—does not account for changes in obligation limitations. The Departments of State and Energy have both security and non-security programs. U.S. Office of Management and Budget, *Budget of the U.S. Government, Fiscal Year 2011, Budget Volume*, Table S-11.

[10] The $10 billion in savings for discretionary programs is in terms of budget authority, rather than outlays. Budget authority is required for programs to spend money; however, no funds are actually spent until an outlay occurs. Effectively, this means that the savings generated by these proposed cuts may not reduce the deficit until future fiscal years.

[11] U.S. Office of Management and Budget, *Budget of the U.S. Government, Fiscal Year 2011, Terminations, Reductions, and Savings*, pp. 1, 3, available at *http://www.whitehouse.gov/omb/budget/fy2011/assets*

[12] President of the United States, *Executive Order—National Commission on Fiscal Responsibility and Reform*, February 18, 2010, available at http://www.whitehouse.gov/the-press-office/executive-order-national-commissionfiscal-responsibility-and-reform

[13] Mandatory outlays were added to discretionary budgetary resources to provide an approximation of total budgetary resources for the purposes of this calculation.

[14] For more information on spending trends, see CRS Report RL33074, *Mandatory Spending Since 1962*, by D. Andrew Austin and Mindy R. Levit and CRS Report RL34424, *Trends in Discretionary Spending*, by D. Andrew Austin and Mindy R. Levit.

[15] There is no standard definition for security and non-security spending. Both the Bush and Obama Administrations have calculated it differently. For FY201 1, the President's *Historical Tables* budget volume, Table 8.1, shows outlays for the non-defense discretionary category at $670.6 billion, whereas the estimates for non-security spending in FY20 11 is $520 billion.

[16] U.S. Office of Management and Budget, *Budget of the U.S. Government, Fiscal Year 2011, Historical Tables*, Table 8.9.

[17] For further explanation, see CRS Report R41097, *The FY2011 Federal Budget*, by Mindy R. Levit.

[18] U.S. Congressional Budget Office, *An Analysis of the President's Budgetary Proposals for Fiscal Year 2011,* March 2010, Table 1-2, available at *http://www.cbo.gov/ftpdocs/112xx/doc11280/03-24-apb.pdf.*

[19] The level of sustainability for the budget deficit cannot be precisely defined. Economists believe that a sustainable budget deficit would be one where the deficit, measured as a percentage of gross domestic product, is lower than the growth rate of the economy. Cumulative budget deficits will cause an increase in the amount of federal spending devoted to net interest costs.

[20] For more information, see CRS Report R40644, *Commerce, Justice, Science, and Related Agencies: FY2010 Appropriations*, coordinated by Nathan James, Oscar R. Gonzales, and Jennifer D. Williams.

[21] Several other agencies are also receiving funding cuts but these are offset by increases in funding to other agencies.

[22] U.S. Congressional Budget Office, *Cost Estimate for the Conference Agreement for H.R. 1*, February 13, 2009, available at *http://www.cbo.gov/ftpdocs/99xx/doc9989/hr1 conference*

CHAPTER SOURCES

The following chapters have been previously published:

Chapter 1 – This is an edited, excerpted and augmented edition of a United States Congressional Budget Office publication, dated June 2010 and revised August 2010.

Chapter 2 – This is an edited, excerpted and augmented edition of a United States Congressional Research Service publication, Report Order Code RL32747, dated January 4, 2010.

Chapter 3 – This is an edited, excerpted and augmented edition of a United States Congressional Research Service publication, Report Order Code R41174, dated April 12, 2010.

INDEX

A

B

C

D

E

I

J

L

M

Q

R

S